6

ENGLISH FOOTBALL

THE COMPLETE ILLUSTRATED HISTORY

Publisher and Creative Director: Nick Wells
Editor: Polly Willis
Picture Research: Gemma Walters and Rosanna Singler
Design: Michael Spender
Production: Chris Herbert and Claire Walker

Special thanks to: Geoffrey Meadon, Sonya Newland and Sara Robson

For Morag, Katy and Elizabeth

FLAME TREE PUBLISHING
Crabtree Hall
Crabtree Lane
Fulham
London SW6 6TY
www.flametreepublishing.com

Flame Tree is part of The Foundry Creative Media Company Limited

Copyright © Flame Tree Publishing

First published 2007

07 09 11 10 08
1 3 5 7 9 10 8 6 4 2

ISBN 978-1-84451-728-2

A copy of the CIP data for this book is available from the British Library.

Printed in China

796.334 JEF

ENGLISH FOOTBALL

THE COMPLETE ILLUSTRATED HISTORY

Author: **ROBERT JEFFERY**   Foreword: **SIR BOBBY ROBSON**

FLAME TREE
PUBLISHING

CONTENTS

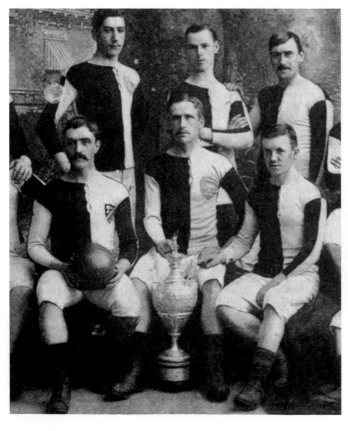

INTRODUCTION

England may be known as the 'birthplace of football', but it certainly was not born there. No matter which ancient civilisation we believe actually began playing a formative version of the game, there is no doubt that it was in England that football was given rules and structure, or that it was English coaches and players who took the game to the rest of the world and made it the most popular global sport, adored by millions.

England's place in the game is special, yet it is possible to treat it with too much reverence: by assuming the country 'owned' the game for many decades, England refused to admit foreign ideas and saw itself overtaken on and off the pitch by foreigners. That mistake has not been repeated: in 2006, foreign players, coaches and investors have been welcomed with open arms into English football.

In almost every way, football is unrecognisable from 100 years ago, and bears only a little relation to even half a century ago, with a very different type of player and supporter, but no amount of change can disguise the very genuine love affair the English public has with the game.

This book chronicles football's rise in England from an elitist pastime which the working classes were deliberately excluded from, to a multi-million pound industry which has permeated every facet of popular culture. It takes in the birth of the Football League and the FA Cup, the first England internationals and the historic World Cup win of 1966, right up to the advent of the Premiership and the incredible changes in the English game since the turn of the twenty-first century.

Any attempt to follow English football history, however, must also examine popular culture, as the two have been inextricably linked ever since the game left the public schools: football's part in aiding the war effort (twice), its effect on the otherwise beleaguered north of the country, and the cultural effects of events as different as the World Cup, the Hillsborough disaster and the hooligan phenomenon mean it has touched the lives of every person in the country, and will continue to do so for many years to come. What began as nothing more than a mere sport has truly become a national obsession.

FOREWORD

FOREWORD

Football in the early years of the twenty-first century remains the highest-profile sport on the planet and its future looks very bright indeed. The continually outstanding standard of football in England, right from the best of the Premier League to clubs to the loyal players of the weekend leagues, demonstrates the enduring popularity of our national game.

All those lucky enough to earn a living from football – including players, managers and those involved in the media – owe a huge debt to the past giants of the sport. The players and managers make today's headlines, but it is the supporters of the game of football that form the bedrock of the sport. It is their passion, their enthusiasm and, ultimately, their money that helps keep the game alive.

Football in this country continues to evolve: the influx of foreign players; sponsorship; mass-media coverage; new stadia; the trend for top clubs becoming Plcs; all this has changed the game radically from its humble beginnings. But nothing can change the fact that to most people, football is more than a game – it is a way of life. It is this fact that should be celebrated – and not forgotten by the biggest clubs.

Many thousands of books on football have been published over the years. Some have been notorious and self-seeking, others well-crafted works of literature. And many excellent reference books, containing all kinds of information and statistics, have been produced.

English Football: The Complete Illustrated History by Robert Jeffery is a worthy addition to the list. It charts the stellar rise of the game in this country, from the days when matches could take up to three days to complete, through the nineteenth century when seismic shifts occurred with the introduction of rules, into the twentieth century and the phenomena of the million-pound footballer, right up to today's complex and thrilling game. It pays tribute to the past and present heroes of the game, and relives some of English football's best – and worst – moments. This is a book to be treasured, as we should treasure our game.

Sir Bobby Robson

Sir Bobby Robson

ORIGINS

Football may not have been the world's first sport – that plaudit probably belongs to archery or wrestling – but it was certainly the first organised team game and is indisputably the sport that has had the greatest impact on modern times.

Tracing football's history can be difficult because there are many variants of the game from ancient times which bear only a slight relation to the game we know today, but it seems most likely that football began in a vaguely recognisable form in China, and later developed as an important ritual in Mexico and other parts of the Americas. Mainland Europe would catch on much later, save for a few matches in medieval France, but it is England which rightly lays claim to being the birthplace of the modern game.

While it was being played all over the world, it was in Britain that it first became a widespread, working-class sport and where rules were first devised to enable everyone to take part as equals.

2,500 BC:
Football In Ancient China

In 2004, world football's governing body, FIFA, formally recognised China as the birthplace of football. Although it is unlikely definitive proof will ever be unearthed, recovered artefacts – in particular balls and drawings depicting early games – suggest that the Chinese played a sport known as *tsu chu* or, more popularly, *cuju* as early as 2,500 BC. This involved kicking an animal skin past 9-m (30-ft)-high bamboo poles and was probably part of military training. The ball would later become round and less likely to burst, and the goals would be made smaller.

By 200 BC, *cuju* had spread to the upper classes and there were even professional players, several of them members of the Chinese royal family, who enjoyed staging *cuju* matches at diplomatic events or feasts. The rules became increasingly complicated, with a points system for performing particular manoeuvres and a number of judges keeping score: matches

A woodblock illustration showing football being played in ancient China.

were watched by thousands of fervent supporters and players gained fame for their exploits on the field. Women were as likely to take part as men, and the game also flourished in Korea and some parts of Japan until medieval times.

c. 1100:
Medieval Football

The first records of a football-like game being played in Britain date back to the twelfth century. It is most likely that football was introduced as a form of military training during Henry I's reign in the early part of the century (1100–35). This was probably known as 'gameball', although the 'game' in question refers to the Old English

word for 'fight' and there were no organised rules.

The object was to get the ball (a pig's bladder sewn tightly together) into the opposition's goal, kicking or punching opponents to get out of the way. The first team to score in this manner would be declared the winner. Military commanders hoped that gameball would get soldiers used to the chaos of the battlefield, and ensure that the strongest came out on top.

With no set pitch size or number of players per team, it was essentially a free-for-all but it still proved popular with those who played it – when they left the military, soldiers took the concept of gameball back to their towns and villages and it evolved into a slightly more organised game.

A game of football in the street in the Middle Ages.

Inflating the bladder of an early Italian football (known as a 'Pallone').

c. 1200:
The Shrovetide Games

Nobody is quite sure when regular Shrovetide 'football' matches began, but most historians date them back to the thirteenth century. They were held across Shrove Tuesday and the following day, Ash Wednesday, and may have originated when a head was thrown into the crowd following an execution.

The Shrovetide football tradition was chaotic and violent, occasionally resulting in death: rival villages would play against each other with the goals up to 5 km (3 miles) apart. Thousands would take part, the game beginning with the pig's bladder ball being thrown into the air at the middle point of the 'pitch'. The two barely organised teams would then push, throw and fight their way to the opponents' goal: games would last into the night and begin again the next day, with the mob rampaging through rivers, forests and villages, trampling everything in its path.

The most famous Shrovetide game, in Ashbourne, Derbyshire, has taken place almost continuously since at least 1683 and draws thousands of competitors to this day, as well as generating considerable media interest. It even gained a royal seal of approval when Prince Charles threw the ball into the air to start the game in 2003.

Football In Literature

Accounts of the increasing popularisation of football during the Middle Ages are hard to come by. We cannot be certain how close they were as a spectacle to the game we know today, but one of the most notable references to the sport – and a major clue that it did indeed involve kicking as one of its main traits – comes in *The Knight's Tale* from Geoffrey Chaucer's *The Canterbury Tales* (c. 1380), where he writes:

'He rolleth under foot, as dooth a ball'.

William Shakespeare would later immortalise the game in his *Comedy Of Errors* (1594):

'Am I so round with you as you with me,
That like a football you do spurn me thus?
You spurn me hence, and he will spurn me hither:
If I last in this service, you must case me in leather.'

Football Is Outlawed

Football may have owed its introduction to Britain in part to the king's armies, but royal approval was hard to come by. Several monarchs disliked football, fearing its popularity among the working classes would make them hard to rule and could lead to more widespread disorder across the country.

In 1314, Edward II issued what is thought to have been the first decree outlawing football when he banned 'hustling over large balls' – his excuse was that local trade was suffering as entire towns and villages chased a pig's bladder across the countryside for days at a time.

Thirty more laws were passed against the game over the next three centuries. Edward III threatened, in 1363, to 'imprison all and sundry' who were found playing 'idle games'. Henry VIII was worried that working time was being wasted on football and banned it in 1540 – a slightly hypocritical approach given that he used to enjoy watching football matches staged in the grounds of Hampton Court Palace.

Edward III banned the game.

Despite all these attempts – or perhaps because of the outlaw reputation they gave footballers – the game continued to flourish across Britain. In Scotland, James IV was known to have played the game himself in the 1500s and even paid a man to fetch balls for him when they were kicked off the pitch.

Football And The English Public Schools

Had football remained strictly a working-class game, it might never have taken off as much as it did during the twentieth century. Without the approval – albeit grudging – of politicians and big business, the game would have remained in the street and might never have gained more widespread popularity.

While many public schools today shun football altogether, it was their involvement in the game in the nineteenth century which paved the way for football to become an important part of wider society. The game was

played at schools such as Eton and Westminster as early as the mid-eighteenth century, but it was never given official approval by the schools' masters and was generally organised by the boys themselves as an impromptu kick-about.

By the 1850s, however, schools had begun to understand that organised sport, particularly team games, could help the boys work off their aggression in a controlled environment and help them learn responsibility and teamwork. Schools such as Harrow, Shrewsbury and Rugby all began to encourage football, allowing older boys

to organise matches under the masters' watchful eyes. Even so, the games themselves were still violent, with frequent 'hacking' or tripping of opponents and occasional riots. In one notable instance in 1818, the army had to be called to deal with a match at Winchester that had got particularly out of hand.

Players wore top hats and later different-coloured caps so team-mates could be recognised, leading to the cap system which players are still awarded for international appearances to this day. Each school played a slightly different variant of the game, with some banning handling altogether and others encouraging it. Some did not play with any sort of offside trap, which led to frequent 'goal-hanging'. This meant that it was impossible for schools to play matches against each other because they could not agree on rules, and when boys left for university or a role in industry they could not form new teams. A single set of rules was to be the final piece in the jigsaw.

Harrow's football team, photographed in 1867.

1860-99

By 1860, football fever was beginning to sweep the country, but the game itself was still disorganised and shambolic. Within the space of the next 30 years, the game would move far closer to the sort of spectacle we enjoy today, with recognisable competitions, star players and tactical clashes between different styles of team.

Fans started flocking to the game and ensured its future success, but football's rise was only possible because of a very definite shift away from the public schools and upper classes and into the mass market. Clubs sprung up all over the country, particularly in the North and Midlands, and the best players would move hundreds of miles to join the best teams, starting an unofficial transfer market which brought about the onset of professionalism.

A definite set of rules, the introduction of the FA Cup and the start of a regular league competition to keep fans and players hooked were all major advances which started in this incredible era of change, overseen by the Football Association which still controls the game in England to this day.

1862:
The (Cambridge) Rules Are Published

Many attempts had been made to establish a single set of football rules between public schools, but agreement had never been reached, hindering the game's development in the wider world. John Charles (J. C.) Thring understood these difficulties only too well – having played football at Shrewsbury as a schoolboy, he wanted to continue the game at Cambridge University but found he could not agree on the basics with his new team-mates, who had been drawn from a number of different schools around the country.

Thring was instrumental in bringing representatives of 14 public schools together in 1848 to devise a set of rules they could stick to – although it took time for them all to come on board. No copy of these original rules – known as The Cambridge Rules – survives, but Thring issued his own rules for what he called 'The Simplest Game' in 1858 and later saw the introduction of a revised Cambridge Rules in 1862, prior to the formation of the Football Association.

Before the rules of football were established, the game was played in open spaces and was something of a free-for-all.

These later rules set out a specific size of pitch and cut down dramatically on touching the ball with hands: they also outlawed tripping. The rules were adopted by most schools, but Blackheath refused to sign up having been unhappy with the handling and tripping rules in particular, and later became a pioneer of rugby union.

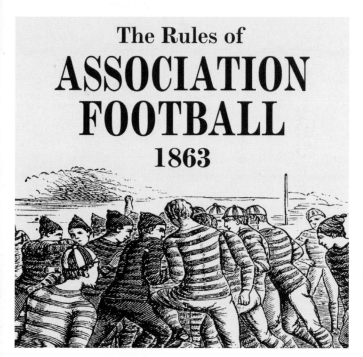

The Rules of
ASSOCIATION FOOTBALL
1863

Shortly after it was established in 1863 the FA issued a book of rules, and the first official FA game was played the following week.

1863:
The Football Association Is Established

When representatives from 15 clubs gathered in the Freemasons Tavern, Great Queen Street, London in October 1863, it is unlikely any of those present would have believed they were witnessing the start of the most important governing body in British football. Yet the Football Association set up that day is the same organisation which still oversees the game in England today and which would become a model for similar associations across the world.

The initial members are far from household names today: they included Kilburn, Crusaders and Kensington School, and all were teams of present or former public schoolboys, a clear indication of where the power in the game initially lay. The main purpose of the first meeting, aside from forming the association itself, was to implement a version of The Cambridge Rules as the official rules for the game in England.

Over the next 20 years, the FA's membership swelled to 50 clubs, but it took its time in exerting genuine influence over the way the game was organised. A week after the rules were finally agreed, the first game was played under official FA jurisdiction, as Richmond took on Barnes at Mortlake, south-west London – it finished goalless and Richmond switched to rugby instead.

FA CUP WINNERS

1872: Wanderers 1-0 Royal Engineers

1873: Wanderers 2-0 Oxford University

1874: Oxford University 2-0 Royal Engineers

1875: Royal Engineers 1-1 Old Etonians
Replay: Royal Engineers 2-0 Old Etonians

1876: Wanderers 1-1 Old Etonians
Replay: Wanderers 3-0 Old Etonians

1877: Wanderers 2-1 Oxford University

1878: Wanderers 3-1 Royal Engineers

1879: Old Etonians 1-0 Clapham Rovers

1880: Clapham Rovers 1-0 Oxford University

1881: Old Carthusians 3-0 Old Etonians

1882: Old Etonians 1-0 Blackburn Rovers

1883: Blackburn Olympic 2-1 Old Etonians

1884: Blackburn Rovers 2-1 Queens Park

1885: Blackburn Rovers 2-0 Queens Park

1886: Blackburn Rovers 0-0 West Bromwich Albion
Replay: Blackburn Rovers 2-0 West Bromwich Albion

1887: Aston Villa 2-0 West Bromwich Albion

1888: West Bromwich Albion 2-1 Preston North End

1889: Preston North End 3-0 Wolverhampton Wanderers

1890: Blackburn Rovers 6-1 Sheffield Wednesday

1891: Blackburn Rovers 3-1 Notts County

1892: West Bromwich Albion 3-0 Aston Villa

1893: Wolverhampton Wanderers 1-0 Everton

1894: Notts County 4-1 Bolton Wanderers

1895: Aston Villa 1-0 West Bromwich Albion

1896: Sheffield Wednesday 2-1 Wolverhampton Wanderers

1897: Aston Villa 3-2 Everton

1898: Nottingham Forest 3-1 Derby County

1899: Sheffield United 4-1 Derby County

1870s:
Formation Of Football Clubs

As football's popularity began to spread beyond the public schools, so clubs were formed in every corner of the country to allow those of all social classes to play, initially in local leagues or unofficial competitions.

The 1870s was the decade when more current professional clubs were formed than any other, although most of those clubs' modern day supporters have little idea how their favourite team began life.

As a general rule, there were three different ways for clubs to start: the church; other sports clubs; and works teams. The church encouraged football since attendance

at services was compulsory for membership of the team. Everton started life in 1878 as St Domingo's, a men's team for the local church. They originally played at Anfield, but when they left the ground their former chairman decided to start a new team to play there: Liverpool can be found there to this day and have generally overshadowed Everton since their formation. Bolton

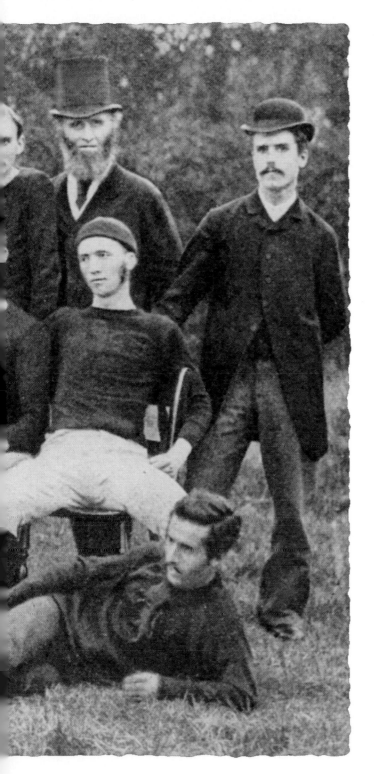

Wanderers were also originally a Sunday-school side in 1874, but severed their ties with the church and moved around the city looking for a permanent home, which earned them their 'Wanderers' tag.

Of those clubs formed from other sports teams, Sheffield Wednesday were a cricket team's way of keeping fit over the winter, Tottenham can be traced back to the Hotspur Cricket Club and both Newcastle and Preston have their roots in cricket and rugby clubs.

Manchester United, meanwhile, are among a number of famous works teams – they were formed in 1878 as Newton Heath by railway employees. West Ham were famously the Thames Ironworks team, hence their 'Irons' nickname, and Arsenal started in Woolwich as a munitions factory club, which is why they are still known as the Gunners. Coventry City were originally called Singer's FC after the well-known bicycle factory their players worked for.

1870:
First Home International

England and Scotland first took the field in March 1870 at London's Kennington Oval, the start of a long international rivalry. The match is regarded as unofficial, since most of the players were FA committee members, and a number of the Scottish team were 'on loan' from the opposition. The match finished 1-1 and the two nations met four more times at the same venue before the first official international game took place between full England and Scotland teams at the West of Scotland Cricket Club in Partick, Glasgow, in November 1872.

It was the brainchild of Charles Alcock, the founder of the FA Cup, who decided that 'in order to further the interests of the Association in Scotland ... a team should be sent to Glasgow to play a match versus Scotland'. Alcock, who was one of the most accomplished centre-forwards of his age, would probably have been selected for the England team himself but was injured and had to be content with a role as an umpire as the game finished goalless.

One of the earliest football teams: Aston Villa in 1879. The 1870s saw more professional teams formed than any other decade in the history of the game. Most of these were formed through church, work or sports groups.

1871:
Start Of The FA Cup

The world's most famous knockout football competition owes its existence to the foresight of the Football Association secretary Charles Alcock, one of the most influential administrators in the game's early years. Alcock realised that a regular competition would create excitement among players and spectators, in the same way challenge matches in schools had when football was first played. So, in the offices of the *Sportsman* newspaper in 1871 he outlined a plan for an official competition for teams from all over the country. Even with official FA backing, only 15 of the association's 50 members decided to enter, compared to more than 600 who take part today.

The first final, held at the Kennington Oval in London, drew only 2,000 spectators who paid a shilling each to see Morton Betts score the winning goal as The Wanderers beat the Royal Engineers 1-0. Alcock, as captain of The Wanderers – a London-based group of former public schoolboys – was the first man to receive the famous cup, and his club would go on to win it three more times before the end of the 1870s. The competition remains as popular today as it ever has been, and is regarded as one of the most romantic and intriguing in sport.

1885:
The FA Legalises Professionalism

With the number of spectators growing, football was becoming a far more serious sport. Club owners, particularly those in the North, were making handsome profits from entrance fees to matches and it was inevitable that clubs would begin offering financial incentives to the best players.

Above: Charles Alcock, father of the FA Cup.

These players were not 'professionals' in the sense that they played football for a living, but the clubs would find other ways to reward them – most notably by securing them well-paid jobs, or in Grimsby's case by offering them a crate of fish. Such practices were rumoured to be common in many of the popular new clubs springing up across the North of England, but many FA councillors and traditionalists were unhappy: they believed that

professionalism would lead to a win-at-all-costs mentality which would ruin the sports' gentlemanly traditions (although some historians argue upper-class administrators were also keen to stop working-class teams succeeding in the sport).

Matters reached a head in 1884 when Preston North End were expelled from the FA Cup after they admitted they had given jobs to nine Scottish players who had moved south to join them. Preston lead around 30 other clubs in threatening to form a separate association of their own, and the FA reluctantly agreed in 1885 that paying players would be allowed providing the players had lived in the area for at least two years and were fully registered with the club.

Blackburn Rovers v. Notts County, FA Cup, Kennington Oval, 1891.

1888:
Start Of The Football League

With 1,000 teams now members of the FA and attendance at the biggest matches as high as 20,000, there was considerable pressure by 1888 for more regular competitive fixtures than the annual FA Cup matches – not least from club owners who wanted a guaranteed regular income to pay their professional players.

The Football League, which copied the format used in county cricket competitions, was the brainchild of William McGregor, a director of Aston Villa. He convened two meetings of leading clubs to discuss his scheme and the first Football League kicked off later that

year with 12 participants: Accrington, Aston Villa, Blackburn Rovers, Bolton Wanderers, Burnley, Derby County, Everton, Notts County, Preston North End, Stoke, West Bromwich Albion and Wolverhampton Wanderers. It is notable that every one of these teams was from the North and Midlands, illustrating just how much professionalism and increasing popularity among the working classes had altered football's landscape.

The League was in existence for more than 100 years, growing steadily in number until the advent of the Premiership saw leading clubs split from the rest of the divisions in 1992, although the Football League name continues to be used to describe the three divisions beneath the Premiership.

Preston North End v. Wolverhampton Wanderers, FA Cup, 1889.

1888/89:
Preston North End's Success

The first season of the Football League was an unprecedented success, with huge crowds across the country, although the opening day itself was something of a disaster: Accrington turned up an hour late for their game with Everton and Stoke had only nine players when they went to Preston. Jack Gordon of Preston is widely regarded as having scored the competition's first ever goal, but some historians claim that match began after the others because of Stoke's difficulties.

Preston were regarded as favourites before the season began and they certainly lived up to that billing, clinching the title by January and eventually finishing 11 points ahead of their nearest challengers, Aston Villa. Most remarkably of all, they did not concede a single match during the entire season, a feat which would not be repeated for another 115 years, when Arsène Wenger's Arsenal team went on an even longer unbeaten run in 2003/04.

Bolton Wanderers, one of the first Football League teams, 1881.

1892:
Division Two Established

Nottingham Forest had been invited to join the original Football League but declined, citing their opposition to professionalism. They soon changed their minds, however, and became founder members of a rival Football Alliance league which drew significant crowds. A friendly between the two leagues resulted in a 1-1 draw, and the Football League decided in 1892 to add the Alliance as its own Second Division.

Two Alliance clubs, including Forest, went straight into Division One, while the others had to vie for promotion. They were: Ardwick, Bootle, Burslem Port Vale, Burton Swifts, Crewe Alexandra, Darwen, Grimsby Town, Lincoln City, Northwich Victoria, Sheffield United, Small Heath (later to become Birmingham City) and Walsall Town Swifts. Promotion and relegation in the early years was a hit-and-miss affair; clubs had to be elected to go up and in some years test matches were held to decide who stayed up and went down. It was not until 1899 that a two-up, two-down system was introduced between the two divisions.

1897:

Opening Of Villa Park, Birmingham

With more spectators than ever before watching the Football League, clubs were investing in enhanced facilities to attract spectators and justify increasing entrance fees. Aston Villa, the most successful team of the 1890s, moved to their new stadium just a week after clinching the league and cup double, and it was quickly recognised as the finest in the country. Built in the grounds of a popular Victorian pleasure gardens, Aston Lower Grounds, Villa Park could hold 18,000 and boasted a brickwork façade and running track.

Although bigger stadiums were to be built during the twentieth century, it remains one of the most atmospheric and popular football grounds in the country to this day and has hosted World Cup finals matches as well as FA Cup semi-finals. The well-known Holte End of the ground is named after Sir Thomas Holte, owner of a nearby stately home.

Division Two team Burslem Port Vale, 1896.

Lord Arthur Fitzgerald Kinnaird (1847–1923)

(Wanderers, Old Etonians, Scotland)

Lord Kinnaird may not have been a footballing superstar in the modern sense, but in the 1870s and 1880s he was as close as anyone came. The Scots-born aristocrat was a passionate player and administrator of the game, and to this day holds the record for the highest number of FA Cup final appearances – nine in all, beginning in 1873. During a lengthy career, he played hundreds of matches in every position on the field, although he was only capped once by his country.

Kinnaird also became the first player to score an own goal, when he carried the ball back over his own line while playing in goal in the 1877 FA Cup final. He spent 50 years as an FA committee member, but was best remembered for his enthusiastic tackling and fine goalscoring record.

Lord Kinnaird (right) – Scottish aristocrat and one of the earliest football superstars – photographed in 1910.

MATCHES

Scotland 0-0 England

Friendly International, Partick, 30 November 1872

Scotland: (Man. n/k) Gardner, Ker, Taylor, Thomson, J. Smith, R. Smith, Leckie, Rhind, MacKinnon, Weir, Wotherspoon

England: (Man. n/k) Barker, Greenhalgh, Welch, Chappell, Maynard, Brockbank, Clegg, Smith, Ottaway, Chenery, Morice

England defeat Scotland 1-0 at the Oval in London, 1972.

The world's first official international match did not receive a huge amount of fanfare, and a relatively disappointing crowd of 4,000 was also adversely affected by the wet weather. Even so, the match had a wider significance as it marked the start of an ongoing football rivalry between the two nations.

The Scottish team was comprised entirely of Queens Park players, with two key men who played in England being deemed ineligible by the English Football Association. England drew most of their team from Oxford University or the fledgling clubs thriving in the London area at the time.

No detailed match report exists of the fixture, but we do know that the Scots generally had the upper hand, and at one point 19-year-old William

FOOTBALL LEAGUE CHAMPIONS

1888/89:	Preston North End
1889/90:	Preston North End
1890/91:	Everton
1891/92:	Sunderland
1892/93:	Sunderland
1893/94:	Aston Villa
1894/95:	Sunderland
1895/96:	Aston Villa
1896/97:	Aston Villa
1897/98:	Sheffield United
1898/99:	Aston Villa
1899/1900:	Aston Villa

Maynard, who had started on the wing for England, switched places with his goalkeeper, Robert Barker. Scotland played in a fluent passing style the English had never experienced before: south of the border, players would run with the ball at their feet until they lost control, while the Scots players worked in pairs to move the ball between them efficiently.

This innovation led to a large number of Scottish players becoming successful in England over the next 20 years, as they exported their ideas to teams such as Burnley, Liverpool and Preston.

The Royal Engineers, 1872–78

Key Players: Major W. Merriman (goalkeeper), Lieutenant R. H. Stafford, Lieutenant H. Renny-Tailyour (both centre-forwards)

Trophies: FA Cup, 1875

There can be no better illustration of just how different the game was in the latter part of the nineteenth century than the Royal Engineers' exploits in the FA Cup in the 1870s. This military corps from Chatham, Kent, made it to three finals, winning the famous trophy once and beating some of the giants of the era in the process.

The Sappers

The Engineers, also known as the Sappers, had joined the Football Association in 1869 and were keen entrants of the inaugural FA Cup in 1871: football was actively encouraged among the Royal Engineers troops, with top brass believing sport was an excellent way to build overall fitness, the lack of which the corps had been criticised for during the 1860s. Members were adept at rugby, cricket and golf as well as football. They made it to the first FA Cup final, where they faced The Wanderers, one of the strongest teams of the time, drawn from the ranks of the leading universities and public schools in the country and boasting six future England internationals in their ranks as well as Charles Alcock, secretary of the FA and the brains behind the competition.

Early Setbacks

The Engineers were further hampered by losing one of their key men, Lieutenant Creswell, after just 10 minutes with a broken collarbone. They lost by a single goal, but were far from finished: in 1874 they again made it to the final, but lost 2-0 to Oxford University.

The Royal Engineers football team, photographed in India in 1860. It was nearly a decade before the team joined the Football Association.

A Team Triumphant

In 1875, they overcame Great Marlow, Cambridge University and Clapham Rovers to set up another meeting with Oxford University in the semi-final. After what is

recorded as a titanic battle, the Engineers triumphed 1-0 and faced the Old Etonians at Kennington Oval for the chance finally to lift the cup. In a high wind, the two teams could not be separated over two hours, drawing 1-1, and a replay was required. This time, the army team emerged triumphant, winning 2-0 thanks to goals from Lieutenant R. H. Stafford and Lieutenant Henry Waugh Renny-Tailyour, the Engineers' key man and one of the most accomplished amateur sportsmen of the day. When the news was relayed to commanding officer General Gallwey at Chatham, he reportedly broke with military protocol by interrupting a parade to toss his cap in the air. The Engineers reached the final again in 1878 but were beaten 3-1 by old adversaries The Wanderers, and as professionalism entered the game they gradually withdrew from national competition.

Preston North End, 1888–93
Major William Sudell

Key Players: N. J. Ross (full-back), Geordie Drummond (wing-back), John Goodall (centre-forward)

Trophies: Football League 1889, 1890, FA Cup 1889

An illustration celebrating Preston North End's successes, 1894.

With three trophies in five years, Preston North End did not exactly dominate the early years of organised competition in England, but the style and off-the-field dedication which they displayed made them the most important and most celebrated team of their era.

Outstanding Manager

Preston were formed in the 1860s and tried a number of sports – including rugby, cricket and lacrosse – without

tasting success before switching to football in 1878. The real masterstroke, and the biggest factor in their future success, came in 1883 when Major William Sudell was put in charge of the first team. Sudell had joined the club as a teenager and played for Preston in many different sports, but he particularly excelled at football and had a flair for organisation and motivation which made him one of the first great managers in the game. Sudell noticed the success Scottish teams were enjoying with the passing game, rather than the dribbling favoured by English sides. He exported a number of Scottish talents, including forward John Goodall, to play alongside local youngsters, and trained his players hard, instilling the virtues of passing in them.

A Winning Streak

The turnaround was swift: North End turned from strugglers to winners almost overnight, and between 1885 and 1886 they were unbeaten in 64 matches, winning 59 of them. They had to survive a scandal when they were thrown out of the FA Cup for employing professionals, a charge Sudell happily admitted. With the rules changed, however, there was little to stop Preston: certainly not Hyde United, who were thrashed 26-0 in 1887, still the biggest victory in a competitive fixture in England. They cruised to the FA Cup final in 1888, but arrogance got the better of them – according to folklore, they asked to have their picture taken with the cup before the match began, so their shirts would not appear dirty in their winners' photograph. They lost 2-1 to West Bromwich Albion, despite dominating the match from start to finish.

'The Invincibles'

Sudell and his players regrouped and returned even stronger in 1888/89, the first year of the Football League. They romped to victory, sewing the title up by January. They also made no mistake in the FA Cup, beating Wolverhampton Wanderers 3-0 in the final in front of a record 22,000 crowd, meaning they became the only team to lift the trophy without conceding a goal in the entire competition and the first team to win the famed 'double' of league and cup. Their remarkable success earned Preston the nickname 'The Invincibles' and they took the league again the following season.

Deepdale

Sadly, changes in the club's hierarchy weakened Sudell's position, and after three successive second-place league finishes he relinquished control. Preston would never again reach such giddy heights, but one thing has remained constant in the Lancashire town – the club's first home, Deepdale, is still where North End take the field every week in the same white shirts Sudell's Invincibles wore.

Well Played "DRUMMOND"

Aston Villa, 1894–97
George Ramsay

Key Players: Jas Cowan (centre-half), John Devey, Charles Athersmith (both forwards)

Trophies: Football League 1894, 1896, 1897 FA Cup 1895, 1897

The second team to do the double, and the last for another 64 years, Aston Villa's side of the mid-1890s was arguably the finest in their history and dominated the English game for three years.

Ramsay Takes Charge

The Birmingham side had enjoyed only modest success in the early years of the league, but the pivotal point in their development was an FA Cup final humiliation against bitter city-rivals West Bromwich Albion in 1892. Villa had beaten Albion in the final five years earlier, but this time they were overpowered 3-0. The defeat

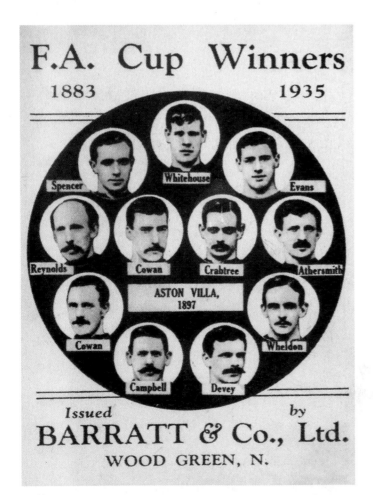

Aston Villa, Cup winners in 1897 – the year they made it a double.

stung secretary and leading light George Ramsay into action, and he began assembling a new team of talented Scottish and northern players, who practiced a new kind of direct, no-nonsense game which shocked more genteel opponents. Ramsay poached trainer Joe Grierson from Middlesbrough Ironopolis and he became the architect of the new-look Villa, assisted by hard-as-nails captain John Devey and super-quick forward Charlie Athersmith.

Swift Revenge

Villa finished six points ahead of Sunderland to clinch the title in 1893/94, but the following season gave them an even greater opportunity – the chance for revenge against Albion in yet another FA Cup final. The teams became the only two sides to face each other in three different finals, and Ramsay was determined his players would not let him down this time. The match was watched by 22,000, many of whom had travelled to London's Crystal Palace Stadium from Birmingham to lend their support. Villa had been preparing for weeks, and their hard work paid off within just 30 seconds, when a Bob Chatt shot deflected off Devey and past the bewildered West Brom goalkeeper. It was the fastest FA Cup final goal of all time, and Villa hung on for the remainder of the match to seal a famous victory – many of their supporters did not even get to see the winner, as the size of the crowd led to delays at the turnstiles getting into the match.

A New Home

Unfortunately, Villa could not hold on to the cup: four months later, it was stolen from the front window of a Birmingham boot manufacturer and the club was fined £25 to pay for a replacement. A local man later admitted stealing it to melt down to make half-crown coins. This setback did not deter Villa, however, and they took the league title again in 1896, before going one better to win the double in 1897, shortly before they moved into their new home at Villa Park. It would be some time before the new stadium tasted the sort of success George Ramsay had brought to the club in the 1890s.

Aston Villa beat West Bromwich Albion 1-0 at Crystal Palace in the 1895 Cup Final.

Making The Rules

For football to thrive, a uniform set of rules was needed and in 1863 the newly formed Football Association gave its backing to the so-called Cambridge Rules, drawn up by Cambridge University and accepted by the leading public schools of the time. The rules helped the game grow and finally saw an end to debates over 'hacking' and handling, with the main advocates of these methods becoming the leading lights in rugby union. Over the years, the rules would be amended many times but always stayed true to the basic principles of the game's formative years – even so, there are many of the 14 Cambridge Rules which seem completely alien to the modern game.

The Cambridge Rules finally put an end to hacking and handling.

The Rules

1. The dimensions of the pitch were set out at 147 x 91 m (150 x 100 yards). Prior to this, there had never been a rule about how large a pitch should be, which led to many arguments, not to mention some extremely large pitches.

2. The goals would be two upright poles, 4.6 m (15 ft) apart from each other. Crossbars were introduced in 1875 and goals were given nets in 1891.

3. The choice of goals would be made by the toss of a coin, and kick-off would take place from the middle of the pitch (although the centre circle itself was not marked out for a number of years).

4. The teams would swap ends at the halfway point of the match, kicking off again from the middle of the pitch. It is worth noting that the numbers of players on each team – although it was generally 11 – and the exact length of the match was left to be agreed between the two clubs.

5. When the ball was kicked forward, any member of the same team closer than the ball to the goal-line was out of play and could not touch it. This was a form of offside rule designed to stop players simply parking themselves next to their opponents' goal-line, but it frequently led to confusion.

6. The ball would be kicked back in when it crossed the touchline, from the point where it crossed the line. Throw-ins were not introduced until 1882.

7. If the ball was kicked behind the goal, the first player to touch it with his hand – from either team – could claim a free-kick to be taken from the goal-line itself. This rule did not survive for long.

8. No player could touch the ball if he was already behind the goal-line at the time it was kicked.

9. A free-kick from either side of the posts would be taken at a point 23 m (25 yards) from the goal on the goal-line itself.

10. At a free-kick, the kickers' team-mates had to stand behind or alongside him, and no opponent could be within 9 m (10 yards).

A *Punch* illustration from 1876, showing Mr Punch kicking a football, in one of the journal's earliest images of the sport.

11. A free-kick could be taken in any manner chosen by the kicker.

12. A goal was awarded when the ball passed between the poles – or when the umpire decided it would have done had the poles been taller. This meant that one could not shoot over the goal; any height counted as a goal.

13. The ball could not be held or hit by the hands, arms or shoulders.

14. Holding, pushing, shinning and tripping were outlawed, but charging at an opponent was still deemed a fair practice.

The Football Association

At a simple meeting in a London tavern in 1863, a blueprint was laid down for the governing body which still controls football in England to this day. The Football Association began life to implement a uniform set of rules and organise competitions, most notably the FA Cup. Today, it has control over the professional and amateur game at every level, and holds the registration details of every player in the country, as well as looking after the England team.

Rising To The Challenge

Over the years, the FA has had to deal with many conflicts and challenges: managing the rise in professionalism; dealing with trade unionism among players; and handling the onset of increasing commercialisation in football. The FA has faced even greater difficulties since the formation of the Premiership, with leading clubs now controlling an overwhelming amount of revenue and power, with the constant threat of a formal breakaway and the ongoing club v country rows over international call-ups.

Twenty years after the competition began, the England team trains for its first World Cup tournament in 1950.

The Formation Of FIFA

One of the most controversial periods in the Football Association's history came in the early part of the twentieth century, when it was approached on a number of occasions by European nations who wanted to hold an international tournament or open discussions about an international football governing body. Each time, the FA failed to see the benefit in taking part in such discussions, believing foreign football to be inferior and competing against other nations to be pointless, so FIFA was formed in 1904 without any representation from the nation which founded the game in the first place.

The Football Association grew out of a meeting in a London tavern in 1863, and it has grown to become one of the most powerful sporting governing bodies in the world.

Their Final Decision?

This us-against-the-world mentality continued even when the first World Cup was organised in 1930, and the British nations declined to take part, with the FA citing the long sea voyage to Uruguay and what they perceived as the second-class nature of the competition. It was not until 1950 that England sent a team to the world's biggest tournament, severely hindering the development of the country's best players. England withdrew from FIFA three times before the Second World War, spending only 18 years as a member between 1906 and 1946, although the FA has been a continuous member since then. A similar attitude saw champions Chelsea advised not to take part in the first European Cup in 1956, but fortunately Manchester United took matters into their own hands and later became the first English side to grace the competition.

1900-18

The final remnants of football's public school origins were shaken off between the turn of the century and the onset of the First World War. Names such as The Wanderers and The Royal Engineers were retreating to the amateur game (where Corinthians were flourishing) and the introduction of a maximum wage legitimised payments to players and led to a huge rise in the number of professional footballers. The best players were becoming celebrities, a fact which angered traditionalists, and transfers between teams for fees became common.

As commercialisation increased, clubs began to build grand stadiums to house their bigger-than-ever crowds, with Arsenal, Manchester United and Chelsea all opening grounds during this era which would become among the best-known in the world. Football even received royal approval in 1914 when King George V attended the FA Cup final. The England team played its first matches on foreign soil as the football bug began to take hold in Europe and South America.

But though the domestic game seemed buoyant, war would prove a major setback to football's rapid progress.

EVENTS

1901:
Maximum Wage Introduced

It might seem a far-fetched idea in today's player-power era, but for the majority of the twentieth century, footballers in England were subject to a maximum wage. The Football League first considered the idea in 1893, but it was voted down; eight years later, however, it was back on the agenda with a vengeance.

One of the main reasons was that in the first 13 seasons of the league, the title had been won 10 times by just three clubs – Aston Villa, Sunderland and Preston. These clubs all had imported Scottish players as key personnel, and had taken players from other First Division sides too, by paying far more than their rivals. Many feared the league was getting predictable and had more to do with financial clout than ability on the pitch. The league duly voted for a cap on wages of £4 per week, and a ban on win bonuses, which effectively meant a level playing-field for every club in the First Division. The £4 limit was reasonably high at the turn of the century, but certain clubs still found ways round the rules by offering gifts or large signing-on fees to new players.

The wage cap stayed in place until 1961, despite a concerted campaign against it by the Players' Union, although it rose far more slowly than the rate of inflation and by the time of its abolition was standing at a relatively paltry £20 per week.

1902:
The Ibrox Stadium Disaster

Stadium safety had never kept pace with the huge growth in football crowds, and to many it seemed only a matter of time before tragedy struck. But the sheer scale of the disaster which took place at Rangers' Ibrox home

The injured are carried from the stands at Ibrox Stadium.

on 5 April 1902 lead to a drastic rethink of the way sport was held throughout Britain.

Seventy thousand fans were watching Scotland play England at the Glasgow ground when, a few minutes into the game, a large section of wooden terracing in the west end of the ground collapsed under the weight of the large crowd, sending many spectators tumbling 12 m (40 ft) to the ground below. Twenty six people died and more than 500 were injured, but amazingly the match still continued as rescue efforts began, and the two sides played out a 1-1 draw. Eye witnesses recalled the stand swaying slightly as late-comers entered the terrace, before it gave way entirely. Wooden terraces were banned as a result of the disaster, and had to be replaced by solid concrete structures; extra attention was also paid to the number of people allowed into a ground, leading to strict capacity limits at large stadiums.

FA CUP WINNERS

1900:	Bury 4-0 Southampton
1901:	Tottenham Hotspur 2-2 Sheffield United Replay: Tottenham Hotspur 3-1 Sheffield United
1902:	Sheffield United 1-1 Southampton Replay: Sheffield United 2-1 Southampton
1903:	Bury 6-0 Derby County
1904:	Manchester City 1-0 Bolton Wanderers
1905:	Aston Villa 2-0 Newcastle United
1906:	Everton 1-0 Newcastle United
1907:	Sheffield Wednesday 2-1 Everton
1908:	Wolverhampton Wanderers 3-1 Newcastle United
1909:	Manchester United 1-0 Bristol City
1910:	Newcastle United 1-1 Barnsley Replay: Newcastle United 2-0 Barnsley
1911:	Bradford City 0-0 Newcastle United Replay: Bradford City 1-0 Newcastle United
1912:	Barnsley 0-0 West Bromwich Albion Replay: Barnsley 1-0 West Bromwich Albion
1913:	Aston Villa 1-0 Sunderland
1914:	Burnley 1-0 Liverpool
1915:	Sheffield United 3-0 Chelsea
1916–18:	No matches during First World War

1904:
Chelsea Move Into Stamford Bridge

London had lacked a major, well-supported team to stamp its name on the football map, but all that was to change with the formation of Chelsea FC in 1904. Almost uniquely in British football, Chelsea were formed to fill an empty stadium rather than simply being formed and then finding somewhere to play. Just as today they are owned by a football-mad businessman, so their entire existence is down to one deep-pocketed entrepreneur.

Property tycoon Gus Mears had owned the Stamford Bridge athletics ground since the 1880s, but when the athletes left he needed a new tenant: nearby Fulham FC, later to become Chelsea's bitterest rivals, rejected the chance, so Mears set about creating his own team, poaching the best talent from bigger clubs and turning Stamford Bridge into one of the best grounds in the country, with a capacity of 100,000. Chelsea (who were almost called London FC) quickly caught the imagination of the capital's fans, with attendances regularly topping 70,000 as they rapidly rose to the First Division.

It would take more than half a century, however, for Chelsea to challenge for serious silverware and even longer to become one of the most successful teams in the country.

Chelsea take on West Bromwich Albion at Stamford Bridge, 23 September 1905.

1907:
Players' Union Is Formed

In 1907, with the maximum wage already in place and the retain-and-transfer system firmly entrenched, professional players decided they ought to stand up for their rights and fight their corner against their clubs and the Football Association.

The original meeting to form the Players' Union was presided over by 'Wing Wizard' Billy Meredith, the best-known player of the day, while Manchester United's Charlie Roberts was elected as the first chair (some believe his work for the union severely restricted his England appearances).

The early union scored a few victories on behalf of individuals in disputes with their clubs and threatened to strike over its right to affiliate to union bodies, but it was not until after the First World War – with a name change to the Professional Footballers' Association – that the union really rose to prominence with the campaign to abolish the maximum wage.

Today, the PFA runs a fund to look after retired players, helps youngsters find work when they drop out of the professional game and steps in to assist when clubs enter administration and are unable to pay wages.

Above: Union president Billy Meredith

A Danish picture of an English footballer.

1908:
England's First Overseas Match

England had already competed against fellow British teams dozens of times by 1908, but they had never kicked off against foreign opposition. In part, this was down to a belief that no foreign team could provide a decent standard of opposition, but it was also due to the difficulties of arranging large-scale foreign travel in the early part of the twentieth century. An FA XI had won three matches in Germany and one in Prague in 1899, but this was an unofficial tour and does not appear in the record books. Nine years later, the FA formally accepted a request to travel to Central Europe for four full internationals.

They kicked off with a 6-1 win against Austria in Vienna, and two days later thrashed the same opponents again 11-1. England then crossed to Budapest to beat Hungary 7-0, before winning 4-0 in Bohemia (later known as Czechoslovakia). The tour was a huge boost to several players' goal tallies, with the Chelsea pair George Hilsdon and Vivian Woodward hitting eight and six respectively – and it also marked the start of a record-breaking run of 10 consecutive wins for England. The level of competition was hardly taxing, but foreign tours soon became regular occurrences.

The gold-medal-winning British team at the 1908 Olympics.

1908:
London Olympics Feature Football

With the Olympics coming to London, it was inconceivable that the national sport would not take place at the world's greatest sporting event. So, for the first time, football was incorporated into the Olympics. Matches were held at White City and Shepherd's Bush,

and eight teams entered, including two from France, and for the first time, a full Great Britain team.

Unsurprisingly, the British were the overwhelming favourites; although all the players had to be amateurs, this technicality still meant that some big names could turn out, including Chelsea's Vivian Woodward, goalkeeper Horace Bailey of Leicester Fosse and Robert Hawkes of Luton, all of whom would also appear for the full England team. Britain crushed Sweden 12-1 and the Netherlands 4-0 before dispatching Denmark 2-0 in the final in front of 8,000 at White City.

Britain took the gold medal again in Sweden four years later, but have not entered a team in the Olympics since 1972 and have not qualified for the final tournament since 1960, fearful that Olympic success would lead to calls for a single British professional team.

1910:
Old Trafford Opens

Newton Heath were renamed Manchester United in 1902, and were soon seeking a new ground to go with their new moniker. The club was enjoying a settled period of financial security after years of turbulence and near-bankruptcy, and the board decided to spend big, bringing in acclaimed stadium architect Archibald Leitch to design a ground in the Trafford area of the city to open in 1910.

The result was Old Trafford, the most spectacular football stadium the country had seen, capable of holding 80,000 with a huge undercover seated area – considered a luxury in those days. The correspondent of sports paper the *Sporting Chronicle* was blown away: 'The most handsomest, the most spacious and the most remarkable arena I have ever seen. As a football ground it is unrivalled in the world.' Bobby Charlton would later famously name it the 'Theatre of Dreams'.

United have played at Old Trafford ever since (save for a period during the Second World War when the ground was bombed and they were forced to share Maine Road with rivals Manchester City), and in their first season there they won the league for only the second time. Today, Old Trafford is the largest club ground in Britain.

1913:
Highbury Stadium Opens

Woolwich Arsenal had enjoyed limited success since forming in 1886 as Dial Square. After problems finding a suitable ground and attracting large enough crowds they decided to make a bold move north of the river in 1913, leasing land in Islington, north London,

Old Trafford, legendary home of Manchester United, as it is now – almost 100 years old.

and constructing a new stadium, known as Highbury. The ground was built over that summer, one of the fastest and most expensive major construction jobs football had seen.

Arsenal had been relegated from the First Division the previous season, but after dropping the Woolwich from their name they regrouped on the pitch in their new ground and were back in the top flight by the time the First World War ended. Highbury was a popular ground, but it got a major facelift in the 1930s and became famous for the marble halls which housed the club's offices inside the East Stand. The whole ground was given Art-Deco styling and even featured in a 1939 feature film, *The Arsenal Stadium Mystery*.

As crowded terraced streets sprung up around it, Highbury became one of the best-known grounds in Britain, but it finally closed its doors in 2006 when Arsenal moved to the nearby Emirates Stadium at Ashburton Grove and is currently being turned into luxury flats.

The Woolwich Arsenal goalkeeper makes a save against Bury at Highbury, 4 October 1913.

PLAYERS

Steve Bloomer (1874–1938)

(Derby County, Middlesbrough, England)

Steve Bloomer was the finest finisher in pre-First World War football and one of the greatest players ever. His ability to put the ball in the back of the net can be seen in his career record of 332 in 525 domestic matches, and his 28 goals in 23 appearances for his country. In an age when attackers needed to be tough, Bloomer's muscular physique and goal-poaching instincts made him invaluable.

He scored four times on his debut for Derby County in 1892 and was top scorer for 14 of his 16 seasons with the club: he spent three years with Middlesbrough but was otherwise loyal to the Rams even though they failed to lift a major trophy. He hit five goals for England against Wales in 1896 and also spent four years imprisoned in Germany during the First World War, having gone there to teach once his playing career ended.

Steve Bloomer, Derby County's – and England's – finest finisher.

Alf Common (1880–1946)

(Sunderland, Sheffield United, Middlesbrough, Woolwich Arsenal, Preston North End, England)

Immortalised in football history as the first-ever £1,000 player, Alf Common was a slightly built but intelligent inside-forward with an excellent record at Sunderland and Sheffield United. He was in his second spell with the former club in 1905 when Middlesbrough, who were looking odds-on favourites for the drop, agreed to pay a four-figure fee for his services. Common kept the team in the top flight, but the move caused huge controversy and led to calls for a cap on transfer fees. A part-time wrestler, Common spent five years with Middlesbrough and also won three England caps, scoring twice.

Inside-forward Alf Common.

William Foulke (1874–1916)

(Sheffield United, Chelsea, Bradford City, England)

Almost certainly the largest man ever to play top-flight football, giant goalkeeper William 'Fatty' Foulke weighed in at 158 kg (25 stone) when he was at his heaviest and gave opposing forwards nowhere to aim at as he filled the goalmouth. Foulke won two FA Cups with Sheffield United and also won an England cap in 1897 – he was a considerable athlete despite his size and an expert at stopping penalties.

Famous Foulke stories include the occasion when he arrived early for breakfast at his team hotel and ate all his Chelsea team-mates' breakfasts, and the day he had to change shirts due to a clash of colours: nothing large enough could be found, so Foulke played the match wrapped in a bedsheet from a local house.

Manchester legend
Billy Meredith.

Billy Meredith (1874–1958)

(Northwich Victoria, Manchester City, Manchester United, Wales)

A colourful and controversial character and a legend in Manchester, Billy Meredith looked set for a life in the mines as his devoutly religious Welsh parents opposed him entering professional football. He eventually persuaded them to allow him to join Manchester City in 1894.

A skilful, free-scoring winger, Meredith won a number of honours with the club and scored both goals as City won 2-0 in the first-ever Manchester derby. In 1909, however, he received an 18-month ban for attempting to bribe an opponent, a charge he always denied. With the ban over, he joined Manchester United but later returned to City, coming out of retirement in 1924 to appear for them in the FA Cup semi-finals at the age of 50.

Chelsea goalkeeper Bill 'Fatty' Foulke.

Sheffield United 1-3 Tottenham Hotspur

FA Cup Final Replay, Bolton, 7 April 1901

Sheffield United: (Man. John Cameron) Foulke, Thickett, Boyle, Johnson, Morren, Needham, Bennett, Field, Hedley, Priest, Lipsham

Tottenham Hotspur: (Man. John Nicholson) Clawley, Erentz, Tait, Morris, Hughes, Jones, Smith, Cameron, Brown, Copeland, Kirwan

Scorers: Sheffield United: Priest 40; Tottenham: Cameron 52, Smith 76, Brown 87

Who are the only non-league team to win the FA Cup? The surprising answer is Tottenham Hotspur, who lifted the trophy in 1901 while playing in the Southern League. The Londoners had not been given an easy draw,

seeing off Preston, holders Bury, Reading and West Brom en route to the final, but even so they were widely expected to be demolished by Sheffield United. More than 110,000 crammed into Crystal Palace for the tie, with 75 separate trains coming from Yorkshire for the big day.

Spurs did themselves credit to draw 2-2 and would have won had the referee not awarded United a goal which film footage later showed had not crossed the line – one of the first-ever video replays. Tottenham, led by player-manager John Cameron and fired by Sandy Brown – who scored in every round of the competition – took revenge in the replay at Bolton, winning 3-1 and leaving United's larger-than-life goalkeeper William Foulke enraged.

Tottenham's Tom Morris runs back on to the pitch after taking a throw-in during the famous FA Cup Replay match in 1901.

Christmas Day 1915 – hostilities cease as troops enter No-Man's Land to play football.

British And German Troops Play In No Man's Land

Friendly International, Belgium, 24 December 1914

For many years, the idea that Allied and German troops in the First World War laid down their arms to play football was dismissed as an urban myth. However, evidence recently unearthed by historians suggests that the events did take place, and on a larger scale than was previously thought.

Troops from both sides had already been in Flanders, Belgium, for a couple of months and losses had been heavy. Both armies had built trenches 2.5 m (8 ft) deep and were anticipating a long and bloody battle, when on Christmas Eve 1914, German soldiers began singing carols. The Allied troops were at first curious, and then began to join in; soon, the Germans were hanging banners which read 'you no fight, we no fight' and offering seasonal greetings. Soldiers began to emerge from the trenches and swapped gifts; some produced makeshift footballs and a number of matches took place.

In all, the ceasefire lasted up to a week, but several commanding officers were unhappy with the situation and shots were fired on occasion – even so, it is a compelling and moving tale.

FOOTBALL LEAGUE CHAMPIONS

1900/01:	Liverpool
1901/02:	Sunderland
1902/03:	The Wednesday
1903/04:	The Wednesday
1904/05:	Newcastle United
1905/06:	Liverpool
1906/07:	Newcastle United
1907/08:	Manchester United
1908/09:	Newcastle United
1909/10:	Aston Villa
1910/11:	Manchester United
1911/12:	Blackburn Rovers
1912/13:	Sunderland
1913/14:	Blackburn Rovers
1914/15:	Everton
1915–18:	League suspended due to First World War

TEAMS

Corinthians, 1882–1939

Key Players: Anthony Hossack (right-half), Arthur Henfrey (forward), Arthur Topham (half-back)

Trophies: No major honours

When discussing the amateur, gentlemanly game which was still thriving at the start of the twentieth century, one name consistently crops up: Corinthians. This famous club embodied the virtues of the public school, but more importantly, introduced football

The Corinthians at a training session at Crystal Palace in January 1923.

to many parts of the world – even getting Real Madrid to change the colour of their shirts.

Preserving Amateur Values

Corinthians were formed in 1882 by N. Lane Jackson. He had two main ideals: to preserve and promote the amateur values he thought were being eroded by the introduction of professionalism; and to bring the best amateur players together in one team, which would train and play together and could provide the nucleus of the England team. With this in mind, Corinthians did not play competitive

fixtures until they decided to enter the FA Cup in 1923; instead, they played friendly matches against many of the finest teams in the land, often winning. They still hold the record for the biggest win over Manchester United, defeating them 11-3 in 1904. The Corinthians players were largely ex-Oxford and Cambridge students and were strictly amateur. Foul play was frowned upon, and the team refused to take penalties because they believed it was ungentlemanly: if they were awarded one, they would deliberately miss and if one was awarded against them the goalkeeper would stand to one side of the goal to allow his opponent to score. In one match, when no referee turned up, legend has it that a Corinthians player refereed as well as playing and even awarded a free-kick against himself.

Spreading The Word

Corinthians were best known, however, for their foreign tours. They went abroad 14 times between 1900 and 1920, spreading the Corinthian message across Europe, the US, Canada, South America and South Africa. In Spain, they played Real Madrid and their opponents decided they would wear white shirts from then on in Corinthians' honour. In Brazil, locals were so enthused they formed a new club named Corinthians which Pele would later play for and which remains one of the country's top sides. In South Africa, they trekked two days by mule wagon to play a match in a remote area. In all, they played 152 tour games and lost only 11.

Corinthian Casuals

It is often said that Corinthians supplied up to nine players for a single England match, but this is a misconception: the Corinthians changed personnel regularly and all their players primarily played for a different club, appearing in Corinthians colours when required. Eighty-three different players with Corinthians affiliations appeared for England, most of them in the late 1890s and early 1900s, but no definite record can be claimed on their behalf. Corinthians merged with Casuals, another successful amateur side, in 1939 and have spent most of the rest of the century in the Isthmian League. Today, they play in Tolworth, Surrey, and various Corinthians teams still tour in honour of their famous forebearers.

The Start Of Professional Football

Many in the game fought against it for years, but with the introduction of the maximum wage professionalism among footballers was on the rise. As the game grew increasingly commercial, average wages rose and it became expected that the leading players would devote all their time to training and perfecting their skills and fitness.

End Of An Amateur Era

The number of amateurs representing England declined steadily in the 1910s, and the final amateur cap was Dulwich Hamlet's Edgar Kail in 1923. By the First World War it was estimated there were more than 4,500 professionals in England at more than 150 clubs, meaning that most Southern and Northern League sides were also paying full-time players as well as their Football League counterparts – in fact, there were more professionals in the country then than there are today.

The 1914 Professional

The footballer of 1914 did not have it quite as cushy as today's stars, however: wages, though respectable, were far from astronomical and the retain-and-transfer system meant that a player could not leave until his club handed over his registration, concentrating the game's power in the clubs' hands. The rule would not be changed for many decades. Players worked hard in training, and with fewer midweek matches were expected to turn up every day and endure extreme physical work-outs.

A medley of famous footballers from the turn of the century.

Supporters pack the stands at the start of a 1912 match between Tottenham and Clapton.

A Living Wage

But for those at the very top of their profession, the rewards were beginning to pick up: a number of clubs experienced brief strikes over wages and bonuses, and there were even reports of agents acting as intermediaries for top players. Big names could endorse brands of cigarettes or foods. The seeds were being sown for the rise of the millionaire professionals which populate the highest levels of the game today, but even so the earnings of the leading professionals did not rise significantly until the maximum wage was abolished in the 1960s. For most of the first part of the twentieth century, players' earnings were not that much greater than the average working wage, which helped foster a greater affinity between players and supporters, who saw the stars as 'one of them' rather than part of an elite. It was still commonplace to see England internationals arriving for First Division matches by public transport as late as the 1960s, for example.

The Sheriff of London Shield, forerunner to the Charity Shield.

Football And The First World War

ootball's role in the First World War is a complex one, shrouded in controversy. While the game acted as a major recruiter for the armed forces during the country's hour of need, there were many who saw football as setting an extremely bad example to young men; indeed, many anti-football attitudes among the middle classes can be traced back to this era.

For King Or Country?

It is significant that King George V became the first monarch to attend an FA Cup final when he watched Burnley beat Liverpool 1-0 at Crystal Palace. The king knew he would need the nation's most popular sport if war did break out. War was formally declared on 3 September 1914, and while most sports immediately called off their championships the Football League decided the 1914/15 season would go ahead as planned. Football was widely criticised, particularly in the popular press, which questioned how young men would be encouraged to fight for their country when they saw their sporting idols apparently ignoring the

1914 FA Cup winners Burnley, who defeated Liverpool 1-0.

The officers play the men of the 26th Divisional Train in Salonika, Christmas Day 1915.

King George V addresses the Manchester City players before the 1933 Cup Final.

conflict. Things grew worse when a number of Liverpool and Manchester United players were banned for match-fixing in 1915: United needed to win the fixture to ease their relegation worries and their 2-0 victory was achieved in extremely suspicious circumstances.

The Footballers' Battalion

The public perception was that football was in fact acting *against* the war effort. The sport's response was to suspend all national competitions from May 1915 and set up a number of more informal regional championships, which required far fewer fixtures and could be re-organised at short notice when players were drafted overseas. The 17th Middlesex Regiment was set up as a 'Footballers' Battalion' and a number of leading players signed up for national service on the pitch at matches to encourage fans

to join suit. At Chelsea, where England international Vivian Woodward was a Footballers' Battalion recruit, a poster read: 'Do you want to be a Chelsea diehard? Join the 17th Battalion of the Middlesex Regiment and follow the lead given by your favourite football players.' All 40 players and staff of Clapton Orient (later to become Leyton Orient) signed up, and three of their players were killed in the Somme in 1916.

Tragic Waste

Football was credited with recruiting half a million men to the forces, and did much to redeem its reputation in the process. The cost, however, was a number of players lost (the number has never accurately been calculated) and much damage to the game's momentum at a crucial period in its development.

1919-38

The period between the two world wars was an exciting one in which to be an English football fan. This was a period of rapid expansion and modernisation both on and off the pitch, and most of all an era of excellent forward play and tactical innovation. Some of the best strikers in English history plied their trade in the 1920s and 1930s: Cliff Bastin and Ted Drake were legends at Highbury, while Dixie Dean broke every record going for Everton.

The England team would surely have been major contenders for the 1930 World Cup had they entered, but a dispute with FIFA prevented that honour being competed for. Domestically, Herbert Chapman became the first genuinely autonomous team manager and lead two different teams (Huddersfield and Arsenal) to three successive titles to become the most celebrated coach of his time. His promotion of team spirit, wing play and fitness would have a major effect on the way the game was played.

The first radio and television broadcasts of football were arguably just as important – although they were very different to the slick productions we enjoy today.

EVENTS

1920:
Division Three Introduced

Harry Johnson.

With a larger number of clubs than ever before employing professionals and boasting stadiums which could accommodate large crowds, it seemed only right to bring even more clubs under the Football League umbrella. A Third Division of the league was introduced for the 1920/21 season, comprising clubs who had been competing in the Southern League, and all but three of its initial 22 entrants are still playing in the professional ranks of the English game to this day: Brentford, Brighton, Bristol Rovers, Crystal Palace, Exeter, Gillingham, Grimsby, Luton, Merthyr Town, Millwall, Newport, Norwich, Northampton, Plymouth, Portsmouth, QPR, Reading, Southampton, Southend, Swansea, Swindon and Watford.

A season later, leading Northern League clubs were added to the Football League family, as Division Three was separated geographically into Third Division (North) and Third Division (South), the champions of each league feeding into the Second Division. The rate of promotion and relegation would

not increase for a number of years, but the structure of the league would remain the same until 1958, when the geographical divisions were removed and a Third Division and Fourth Division created.

1923:
Wembley Stadium Opens

Wembley is today synonymous with football, but it was originally built to house the British Empire Exhibition, a stunning showcase of Britain's interests around the world which was planned for 1924. The government chose the site of a golf course in north-west London for the new Empire Stadium, largely for its strong transport links with the new Metropolitan line stopping nearby. Construction lasted 300 days and cost £750,000, with thousands of people hired to simulate the way a football crowd would behave by jumping up and down simultaneously to test the stadium's construction.

King George V opened Wembley in time for the infamous 1923 FA Cup final, and it immediately acquired legendary status due to its size and splendour. More than 24 million people would visit the Empire Exhibition, but the Football Association was initially slow to see Wembley's potential as a football stadium. It was used for cup finals but the England team continued to move around the country, and only after the Second World War did it become the permanent home of the national side.

England first played there in 1924, when they drew 1-1 with Scotland in a half-empty stadium. Wembley's famous Twin Towers were the backdrop to England's spectacular 1966 World Cup victory and sealed the stadium's place in footballing folklore; these were knocked down in 2002 as demolition work began to replace the stadium with a new ground fit for the twenty-first century.

The first Wembley FA Cup Final – West Ham United v. Bolton Wanderers.

FA CUP WINNERS

1919:	No matches during First World War
1920:	Aston Villa 1-0 Huddersfield Town
1921:	Tottenham Hotspur 1-0 Wolverhampton Wanderers
1922:	Huddersfield Town 1-0 Preston North End
1923:	Bolton Wanderers 2-0 West Ham United
1924:	Newcastle United 2-0 Aston Villa
1925:	Sheffield United 1-0 Cardiff City
1926:	Bolton Wanderers 1-0 Manchester City
1927:	Cardiff City 1-0 Arsenal
1928:	Blackburn Rovers 3-1 Huddersfield Town
1929:	Bolton Wanderers 2-0 Portsmouth
1930:	Arsenal 2-0 Huddersfield Town
1931:	West Bromwich Albion 2-1 Birmingham
1932:	Newcastle United 2-1 Arsenal
1933:	Everton 3-0 Manchester City
1934:	Manchester City 2-1 Portsmouth
1935:	Sheffield Wednesday 4-2 West Bromwich Albion
1936:	Arsenal 1-0 Sheffield United
1937:	Sunderland 3-1 Preston North End
1938:	Preston North End 1-0 Huddersfield Town

1923:
The Football Pools

John Moore's (later to become Littlewoods) began a national obsession when they handed out 4,000 pools coupons to Manchester United fans at Old Trafford in 1923. The pools would become big business, handing out £3 billion in prize money over the next 80 years, including £3 million in one single week during 1988. There are a number of variations of the game, but the basic idea is to choose correctly matches from a Saturday's English and Scottish fixtures which will be draws: points are awarded for each correct draw, and reaching a certain number of points overall brings a payout.

The game grew in popularity, attracting 15 million entries at its peak, thanks to the lack of other legalised lotteries and the idea that one could use footballing knowledge to gain an upper hand. From the 1970s onwards, a certain percentage of pools money went back into the game, often to pay for stadium refurbishments or community schemes. Since 1994, however, the pools has been in decline, with the National Lottery taking the lion's share of its income.

The Littlewood's pools – originally John Moore's – was big business almost as soon as it began in 1923.

The successful Huddersfield Town team of the 1920s, photographed in October 1925

Britain's most famous pools winner was Viv Nicholson, a poverty-stricken mother-of-three from Castleford who landed £150,000 in 1961 but soon spent the lot, inspiring a stage musical called *Spend, Spend, Spend.*

1926:
Huddersfield's Success

Huddersfield's magnificent achievement in winning three league titles in a row was all the more remarkable given just how poor a state the club had been in before their transformation. Debt-ridden and deeply unfashionable, the Yorkshire side were never expected to be title contenders, but all that changed dramatically with the appointment in 1920 of Herbert Chapman as manager.

Chapman had only just recovered from the scandal which had engulfed his former club, Leeds City – the club had been dissolved and the players auctioned off in a hotel after illegal payments were found – and had spent time out of the game managing a factory when he became involved with Huddersfield, first as secretary and then as manager. Chapman's famous motivational skills and eye for a bargain transformed the side, and they lifted the FA Cup for the first time in their history in 1922, beating Preston 1-0.

Their first-ever championship, in 1924, was achieved by the slimmest of margins; on the final day, Huddersfield needed to beat Nottingham Forest by three goals and hope Cardiff did not win in order to clinch the title. Town won 3-0 to keep up their end of the bargain, and Cardiff missed a penalty in the final minute as they were held to a goalless draw. Things were easier next time around, and Huddersfield were unbeaten for 17 games en route to the title. By the time they made it a hat-trick, Chapman had left for even more success at Arsenal.

1927:
First Match
Broadcast On Radio

The first World Cup. The teams for Uruguay and Argentina wave to the crowds before the match starts. It ended with victory for the host nation Uruguay.

Football's broadcasting debut was made possible because the BBC received a Royal Charter in 1927, giving it a public service remit and a licence to cover major sporting events. Football first hit the airwaves when BBC Radio covered the Arsenal v Sheffield United clash from Highbury on 22 January that year.

Former rugby player Henry Blythe Thornhill Wakelam was the first-ever football commentator, and the match finished 1-1. Nervous producers had been unsure how listeners would follow the action, so they printed a diagram of a pitch in the *Radio Times*, divided up into

numbered squares. A co-commentator would call out the number of the square the ball was in, so those at home could visualise where the action was taking place; it is believed this practice explains the origin of the phrase 'back to square one'.

The broadcast was considered a major success, and led to regular commentaries from leading matches. That year's cup final was also broadcast on the radio, as Cardiff took the trophy out of England for the only time, beating Arsenal 1-0 with a freak goal which goalkeeper Danny Lewis spilled over the line following a tame shot.

1930:
First World Cup Finals Tournament

Had England entered the first-ever World Cup tournament they would probably have been favourites, and might have taken the famous trophy home with them. Certainly, broadening English football's horizons by exposure to high-level international competition would only have been a healthy experience, but the first-ever World Cup took place without the country which had invented and popularised the sport in the first place.

All the Home Nations were in dispute with FIFA in 1930, and had temporarily withdrawn their membership of the world game's governing body in protest at payments to amateur players. FIFA intended the World Cup to be the perfect showcase for the game's new global appeal, but their decision to hold the first tournament in Uruguay was a strange one: while football was certainly soaring in popularity in South America, and Uruguay themselves were the reigning Olympic champions, the lengthy sea voyage put many European nations off entering, and in the end only 13 teams took part in the tournament. The hosts beat Argentina 4-2 in the final.

One Englishman did make it to the tournament, however: Liverpool-born George Moorhouse had left the UK in 1932 after a couple of appearances for Tranmere Rovers and ended up playing for the New York Giants and appearing for the American team which reached the World Cup semi-finals.

1936:
Joe Payne

Joe Payne was a fairly unremarkable wing-half who was in and out of the Luton Town team in the Third Division (South) in 1936. On Easter Monday that year, however, he wrote his way into the record books. Injuries meant Payne was forced to play up front against Bristol Rovers and he scored 10 goals as his team won 12-0.

It is still the largest personal haul in senior British football to this day, and it is fair to say Payne kept his place at centre-forward from that day on. The next season, he scored 55 goals as Luton romped to the title, and in 1937 he won an England cap, scoring twice in an 8-0 win against Finland: despite this, he never made a second appearance for his country. Payne went on to play for Chelsea and West Ham before the Second World War brought an end to his career.

1937:
First Match Broadcast On Television

Just as Highbury had been the venue for the first radio foray into football, so Arsenal's home was also the venue when the sport was broadcast on television for the first time in September 1937. Cameras made a live broadcast of parts of a match between the Arsenal first team and the reserves, mainly as an experiment to see quite how difficult broadcasting live football would be: although there were many logistical problems during the broadcast, the BBC got better at football as the season progressed and both the England team and the FA Cup final were featured live during 1938.

Left: Luton Town's Joe Payne. Right: Preston North End's Tom Smith clasps the FA Cup.

PLAYERS

Arsenal's Cliff Bastin.

Cliff Bastin
(1912–91)

(Exeter City, Arsenal, England)

Cliff Bastin's goalscoring achievements were all the more remarkable given that he was almost entirely deaf. The Devon-born striker is one of Arsenal's greatest forwards of all time and might have hit even more had the Second World War not interrupted his career. Bastin started out with hometown club Exeter as a 16-year-old, but his potential was quickly spotted by Arsenal manager Herbert Chapman, and after joining the Londoners in 1929 he never left.

He scored 150 times in the league and 178 times overall, both records which stood for more than 50 years. He also scored 12 goals for his country. Unable to fight in the war due to his disability, Bastin spent the conflict as a warden stationed on top of Highbury.

Raich Carter (1913–94)

(Player: Sunderland, Derby County, England; Player & Manager: Hull City; Manager: Leeds United, Mansfield Town, Middlesbrough)

A free-scoring inside-forward, Raich Carter won major medals at every club he played for, and had captained Sunderland to both the FA Cup and league title by the time he was 24. He went on to repeat his success with

Sunderland captain Raich Carter holds up the FA Cup in front of his team-mates and directors at King's Cross Station.

Derby, who he joined in 1946, winning another FA Cup to become the only player to do so both sides of the war. Carter also played 13 times for England, scoring seven goals.

As a manager, he led Leeds to the top flight but surprisingly was released by the club and enjoyed little success with Middlesbrough in the 1960s. He is best remembered, however, as an inspirational captain and model professional.

Herbert Chapman.

Herbert Chapman
(1878–1934)

(P: Grimsby, Northampton, Sheffield United, Notts County, Tottenham; M: Northampton, Leeds City, Huddersfield Town, Arsenal, England)

Herbert Chapman can lay claim, among other things, to being the first genuine manager in the British game. At Huddersfield and Arsenal, he achieved autonomy in transfers and team selection, whereas previously managers had merely been glorified coaches, deferring to the board of directors in all matters. Chapman's tactical awareness and coaching skills changed the British game and ushered in a new era of professional training for top-flight clubs.

After an unremarkable playing career and only minor success with Northampton and bankrupt Leeds City, Chapman turned unfashionable Huddersfield into three-times league champions and later repeated the remarkable feat with Arsenal (indeed, the club's red kit was his idea). He was the first individual to manage the England team, for one match in 1933, but he did not pick the players.

William 'Dixie' Dean
(1907–80)

(Tranmere Rovers, Everton, Notts County, England)

Few strikers can boast an almost goal-a-game scoring record throughout their career, but Everton legend Dixie Dean was no ordinary forward. Brave, hard-working and truly professional, Dean found the back of the net with remarkable regularity during a 16-year career, most of it spent at Goodison Park.

Dean joined Everton as an 18-year-old in 1925 for the modest sum of £3,500 and went on to score 383 goals in 433 appearances for the club, including 60 in the 1927/28 season alone and 16 more for England. He stayed with the club despite their relegation in 1930 and fired them back to the top flight. A legend with the Toffees, Dean died in 1980 while watching the Merseyside derby.

Everton's Dixie Dean (left) shows his skill.

Ted Drake (1912–95)

(P: Southampton, Arsenal, England; M: Reading, Chelsea)

The first man to win the Football League title as both a player and a manager, Ted Drake is a legend at two London clubs: Arsenal and Chelsea. After joining the Gunners as a player in 1934, he scored 139 times; his 44 goals in all competitions during the 1934/35 season are still a club record and helped bring the championship to north London.

As a manager, Drake transformed Chelsea from also-rans to champions in 1955 by bringing in an entirely new squad and completely revamping training methods. He was sacked in 1962 after failing to secure further silverware at Stamford Bridge.

Hughie Gallacher (1903–57)

(Queen Of The South, Airdrieonians, Newcastle United, Chelsea, Derby County, Notts County, Grimsby, Gateshead, Scotland)

Newcastle's number nine shirt has become one of the most famous in football down the years, but Hughie Gallacher was the man who started the ball rolling. He first donned the jersey in 1925 after a prolific career in Scotland, and scored 143 times in five years to become a Tyneside legend – all the more remarkable given that he stood at only 1.6 m (5 ft 5 in). He captained the Magpies to the title in 1927 with 36 goals, but was unable to repeat his success during a later spell with Chelsea. Beset by personal problems and court appearances, he threw himself in front of a train in 1957.

Left: Arsenal's Ted Drake, photographed in 1930.

Right: Newcastle's Hughie Gallacher, 1930.

Wilf Mannion (1918–2000)

(Middlesbrough, Hull, England)

Middlesbrough's greatest-ever player and a long-time servant of the club, Wilf Mannion was a mesmerising dribbler of the ball and a notable ambassador for North East football. He played 368 times for Boro over 18 years and also made 26 appearances for England, scoring a hat-trick on his debut against Northern Ireland in 1946. Stanley Matthews was often compared to Mannion, but the latter's finishing was arguably even better – he scored 110 times for Middlesbrough during his career. He came out of retirement to spend a season with Hull and played in non-league into his forties.

Alex James (1901–53)

(Raith Rovers, Preston North End, Arsenal, Scotland)

An intelligent and unselfish inside-forward famed for his baggy shorts, Alex James was a very modern footballer who supplied the ammunition for many of Arsenal's fine achievements in the 1930s. After building his reputation with Raith Rovers in Scotland and later Preston, James became a vital part of Herbert Chapman's Arsenal revolution when he joined the club in 1929. He won the league four times and the FA Cup twice and was also part of the Scotland team which shocked England by winning 5-1 at Wembley in 1928 (although he won only eight caps in total for his country). He went on to become a notable newspaper journalist.

Above: Arsenal's Alex James, January 1935.

Right: Middlesbrough's Wilf Mannion, 1949.

MATCHES

Bolton Wanderers 2-0 West Ham
FA Cup Final, Wembley, 20 April 1923

Bolton: Pym, Haworth, Finney, Nuttall, Seddon, Jennings, Butler, Jack, J. R. Smith, J. Smith, Vizard

West Ham: Hufton, Henderson, Young, Bishop, Kay, Tresadem, Richards, Brown, Watson, Moore, Ruffell

Scorers: Jack 2, J. R. Smith 53

The first FA Cup final to be played at Wembley went down in history more for off-the-pitch happenings than the game itself. It was the stadium's grand opening, and although 123,000 could be accommodated (and indeed, that is the official attendance given for the match) the curiosity of the general public about what had been billed as a masterpiece of sporting architecture meant that up to 200,000 crammed into Wembley.

The match threatened to descend into farce, but with the king looking on an abandonment could not happen: the crowd was spilling onto the edges of the pitch and players could not take run-ups to corners or throw-ins. It was said that a member of the crowd kept the ball in play at one point and that a West Ham defender was held up by supporters as he tried to get back to stop Bolton's second goal. The match became known as the White Horse Final, because PC George Scorey rode Billy, a white police horse, to drive the crowd back before kick-off, one of the most famous images in football history. England international David Jack and Jack Smith scored Bolton's goals as they emerged 2-0 winners.

Walsall 2-0 Arsenal
FA Cup Third Round, Walsall, 14 January 1933

Walsall: Cunningham, Bennett, Bird, Reed, Leslie, Salt, Coward, Ball, Alsop, Sheppard, Lee

Arsenal: Moss, Male, Black, Hill, Roberts, John, Warnes, Jack, Lambert, James, Bastin

Scorers: Alsop, Sheppard (pen)

The greatest day in Walsall's history, and the first-ever FA Cup 'giantkilling', Arsenal's defeat in 1933 still ranks alongside the competition's finest moments to this day.

Herbert Chapman's Gunners had reached the final the previous year and finished second in the First Division, and they would go on to win the 1933 championship. With the likes of Cliff Bastin and Alex James in their ranks, as well as three other internationals, they were arguably the finest team in the land.

Walsall, by contrast, were struggling in the Third Division (North). However, the Midlands team tore into their opponents with ferocious enthusiasm from the very first minute, and after holding them goalless to the break, Walsall took the lead through their legendary forward Gilbert Alsop early in the second half. Tommy Black then gave away a needless penalty and Bill Sheppard settled the tie from the spot. Walsall were carried off the pitch as heroes, and Black was banned from Highbury by a furious Chapman and later transferred to Plymouth.

Captains George Kay and Joe Smith at the 1923 FA Cup Final.

FOOTBALL LEAGUE CHAMPIONS	
1919/20:	West Bromwich Albion
1920/21:	Burnley
1921/22:	Liverpool
1922/23:	Liverpool
1923/24:	Huddersfield Town
1924/25:	Huddersfield Town
1925/26:	Huddersfield Town
1926/27:	Newcastle United
1927/28:	Everton
1928/29:	Sheffield Wednesday
1929/30:	Sheffield Wednesday
1930/31:	Arsenal
1931/32:	Everton
1932/33:	Arsenal
1933/34:	Arsenal
1934/35:	Arsenal
1935/36:	Sunderland
1936/37:	Manchester City
1937/38:	Arsenal
1938/39:	Everton

TEAMS

Arsenal, 1930–38

Key Players: Cliff Bastin (forward), Alex James (inside-forward),
Frank Moss (goalkeeper)

Trophies: Football League 1931, 1933, 1934, 1935, 1938; FA Cup 1930, 1936

There were many factors which led to Arsenal's remarkable success in the 1930s, but by far the single greatest influence was manager Herbert Chapman. He revolutionised the club and gave it a platform for decades of success. It is no surprise that a bronze bust of the great man stood proudly in the entrance at Highbury after his death, and moved to the Emirates Stadium with the club in 2006.

Chapman's Champs

Chapman took over in 1925 on a salary of £2,000 per year, making him the best-paid manager in the game. He had already worked wonders with Huddersfield, leading them to three titles in a row, and would display the same magic in north London. It took a while, though, to turn around the fortunes of a club which had achieved little on the pitch save for holding on to First Division status. Chapman built a strong team spirit, and spent £25,000 – a huge sum in those days – recruiting a number of brilliant individuals, from deadly forward Cliff Bastin and incisive inside-forward Alex James to left-back Eddie Hapgood, who was spotted playing for Kettering Town while working as a milkman and went on to captain England.

Innovative Instinct

Chapman had an eye for picking up those overlooked by other clubs and moulding them into champions, and he also introduced a number of significant innovations to the game, including floodlights, numbers on shirts and white balls. After losing the 1927 FA Cup final to Cardiff, Arsenal won 2-0 in 1930 in a grudge match with Huddersfield famous for a Graf Zeppelin flying over the pitch. The following year, the Gunners cruised to the league title, scoring a remarkable 127 goals in the process.

Record Success

In 1933, the club began a run of three consecutive championships, but just as at Huddersfield Chapman had been unable to see out the third of his league titles, so at Arsenal he was absent from his record-equalling moment of triumph, this time, because he died in 1934, stricken by pneumonia after attending a reserve match against doctor's orders. George Allison picked up the reins and carried on Chapman's good work, adding an FA Cup in 1936 and another league title in 1938 to make an incredible total of seven trophies in eight years. The Second World War interrupted the club's momentum and robbed Arsenal of nine players, but their place in the record books was already assured.

The 1931 Arsenal team, showing off their silver. Manager Herbert Chapman sits three from left in the front row.

Everton, 1928–39

Key Players: Dixie Dean (centre-forward), Ted Critchley (winger), Ted Sagar (goalkeeper)

Trophies: Football League 1928, 1932, 1939; FA Cup 1933

While Arsenal's success was based around a visionary manager, Everton's many achievements in the pre-war era could not have come from a more different source.

Dynamic Dixie

Unlike most top-flight clubs, which had begun to give control to individual managers and coaches during the 1920s, the Merseysiders resisted appointing a manager until 1939; instead, the team was picked and transfers were made by committee. The one person who was often consulted, however, was record-breaking centre-forward William 'Dixie' Dean – and it is to he that most of Everton's trophies during that period can be attributed. There is no such thing as a one-man team, but Dean-era Everton were lost when their talismanic striker was absent, and the fact they did not win more trophies during this period can be put down to the regular struggles with injury Dean endured.

Predatory Instincts

Dean joined the club from Tranmere in 1925, but a motorcycle accident months later almost ended his career: he was unconscious for 36 hours but made a full recovery and two years later led the Toffees to the title, scoring 60 goals to set a new league record – including all five in a 5-2 victory over Manchester United. Dean was a nightmare for opposing defenders: unbeatable in the air, his predatory instincts and constant movement were impossible to handle. Backed by stalwart goalkeeper Ted Sagar, a Scottish back-line that formed a virtually impenetrable wall in defence, and the constant supply line of winger Ted Critchley, only Arsenal could match the Blues during this period.

Top Toffees

In 1930, the club were relegated after a shocking run of results and some bad moves in the transfer market, but they regrouped and returned to the top flight, winning the title again in their first season back. Everton scored 116 goals en route to the 1932 championship, even though Dean did not find the net for the first six games of the season, sparking fears of a crisis. Manchester City were dispatched 3-0 at Wembley in 1933 to take the FA Cup to Merseyside. Dean had retired by the time Everton lifted the title again in

Everton's 1931 team: standing (l-r): McClure, Gee, Coggins, Thomson, Cresswell and H. Cooke (trainer). Seated (l-r) Critchley, Dunn, Dean, Williams, Johnson and Stein.

1939, but the club found the perfect replacement in Tommy Lawton, who was signed from Burnley and immediately started scoring so regularly he went straight into the England team. Lawton hit 34 goals that season, but his Everton career was hampered by the war, as was the rest of that title-winning team. At least they can claim to have held on to a championship trophy longer than any other club – for seven years from 1939 to 1946, the silverware was securely locked away at Goodison Park.

The Broadcasting Of Football

Football and broadcasting have endured a difficult relationship over the years: while they undoubtedly need each other, there has been constant friction between the two camps and to this day many believe television has done more harm than good to the English game.

Hitting The Airwaves

Radio was, naturally, the first form of football broadcasting, but it had to survive a 14-year ban which began in 1931 when smaller clubs started complaining that live radio coverage of big matches was hitting their attendances. It was the first of many such arguments down the years, but radio coverage has since become omnipresent, with the 5pm results round-up on the BBC a popular ritual among fans. Television proved a more controversial medium. The first broadcasts in 1938 were popular, but even so the game was only an occasional guest on the nation's screens for the next 15 years. With only one channel at the time, the BBC could not justify showing two hours of live football very often, and the Football League did not give permission for live matches to be shown until the 1980s. That left just the FA Cup and England internationals, and even this proved

BBC TV cameras film the FA Cup Final between Manchester United and Blackpool in 1948.

A Sky Sports cameraman gets up close and personal with Tottenham Hotspur's Robbie Keane.

controversial: the reason the FA Cup final was moved to the week after the league season had ended was because clubs believed the television audience was adversely affecting their attendances.

Match Of The Day

Two major factors helped popularise television football: technology and the World Cup. Advances in broadcast technology made it possible for the first time for match footage to be delivered to a studio for editing and replaying in a matter of hours: the result was *Match Of The Day*, launched by the BBC in 1964 to show extended highlights of the best league fixture of each Saturday. It became a popular Saturday-night ritual, presented by Kenneth Wolstenholme and later Jimmy Hill, with viewers able to enjoy bite-sized chunks of football without the worry of missing out on live Saturday afternoon action (to this day, English law forbids the televising of Saturday afternoon matches for this very reason). *Match Of The Day* became a wider highlights

show, and survived an audacious 'Snatch Of The Day' in the late 1970s when ITV entered the fray and attempted to outbid the BBC for the rights to Football League action. The two channels were eventually allowed to share a small number of live games. The 1966 World Cup, which was fully televised, led to a surge of interest in football and vastly increased viewing figures; 1970's tournament was shown in colour and arguably had an even greater effect.

The Digital Age

The next major milestone in broadcasting was the creation of the Premier League in 1992, which saw live match rights sold to satellite broadcaster BSkyB; only Sky now shows live Premiership games, although *Match Of The Day* survives and the FA Cup and England matches are still largely the domain of terrestrial channels. The next broadcasting battle is likely to take place on an even smaller screen, as the right to show highlights on mobile phones becomes an increasingly lucrative market.

Bristol Rovers goalie Ellis just manages to save the shot from Charlton's Robinson, 1935.

League Divisions

With the introduction of a Third Division in 1920, splitting into North and South the following year, the make-up of the Football League was set for the next 40 years.

Two-Up, Two-Down

During that time, promotion and relegation became standardised: two-up and two-down between the First and Second Divisions with the two Third Division champions taking their place in Division Two. Clubs finishing bottom of the Third Divisions would apply for re-election and were generally successful: after the Second World War, most of the teams leaving the Football League did so through bankruptcy (Accrington Stanley, Aldershot, Maidstone) with only a few failing to gain enough votes from fellow clubs to stay up (Bradford Park Avenue, Barrow, Southport).

Play-Offs

From 1987, the champions of the Conference were automatically promoted if their grounds met size and safety criteria, and today two clubs go up to the league proper, one as champions and one via the play-offs. From 1960, the two Third Divisions became Divisions Three and Four with an end to regionalisation, and the rate of promotion increased gradually over the years; three up and down between the top two divisions and four in the lower two. There have been regular calls over the past 20 years for the two bottom divisions to be regionalised once more, to cut down on travelling costs and increase the number of money-spinning local derbies clubs take part in. From 1981, three points were awarded for a win to reward attacking play, and in the late 1980s play-offs were introduced to decide promotion matters: they remain in use in all Football League divisions today as a way of separating those sides who finish below the automatically promoted champions and runners-up.

Changes In Name Only

The old First Division is today named the Premiership, and is administrated differently from the other divisions although it remains under the FA's jurisdiction; in 2004/05 what was by then known as the First Division (but was in fact the old Second Division) was renamed the Championship, with the divisions below it becoming League One and League Two in the latest of a series of confusing name changes and alterations to league structure which did not, in reality, make any significant difference to the leagues' format.

Fulham team members celebrate their 2001 promotion to the Premier League.

1939-59

The onset of war called a halt to a game in the ascendancy, but the way football kept on playing in the face of adversity, as well as supplying many heroes to the armed forces, did much to raise the level of goodwill surrounding the game. Any doubts over English football's ability to bounce back from six years of erratic competition were dispelled as soon as the 1946/47 season kicked off to record attendances, and in almost all respects the post-war era was a boom period. England entered the World Cup for the first time in 1950, although the results were not as favourable as they might have hoped, and Wolves played a series of friendlies against notable foreign opposition as the English game became less insular and began to acknowledge it could learn much from the Europeans and South Americans. Hungary's shocking defeat of England at Wembley in 1953 played a large part in this, bursting England's bubble of superiority once and for all and exposing English coaches and players to new tactics and ideas.

The European Cup helped further the horizons of the country's leading clubs, but it also led to one of the worst tragedies to befall the game, as the talented 'Busby Babes' of Manchester United were decimated in an air crash in Munich in 1958.

EVENTS

1946:
Burnden Park Tragedy

Just as English football was starting to get back to normal following the war, disaster struck. The FA Cup had reached the quarter-final stage, with matches being played over two legs: Stoke, including the legendary Stanley Matthews, were trailing 2-0 when they visited Burnden Park, Bolton, for the second leg. The match had created huge interest locally, and attendances across the country had been high as people enjoyed sport again with the war finally over.

Bolton had been expecting a crowd of 65,000 but it is estimated that 20,000 more than that turned up, many clambering over railings to get into the ground for free. The crowd did not disperse evenly around the stadium, and supporters became crushed against steel railings in the Bolton End. The crowd began to spill onto the pitch, and dead and injured spectators were carried away – most of those left in the ground were unaware that 33 people had died until they heard about it on the radio or saw it in the newspapers later, as the players had been ordered to restart the game.

A number of new safety measures were put in place as a result of what happened, and the events overshadowed what was one of the most thrilling title races for years, as Liverpool grabbed the honours on their final day of the season – they had to wait two weeks to see if Stoke would win their last game and overtake them, and were relieved when the Potters lost 2-1 to Blackpool.

1950:
England's First World Cup Finals

The Home Nations ended their long-running dispute with FIFA in time to enter the 1950 World Cup, and following the appointment of Walter Winterbottom as England's first full-time manager there was every reason to be optimistic leading up to the finals.

Winterbottom, one of the game's leading thinkers, put a proper coaching infrastructure in place to nurture young English talent, and on the pitch he led England to a 10-0 thrashing of Portugal and a 4-0 win in Italy in 1948. England qualified by winning the 1949 Home Nations title, and went into the finals in Brazil as one of the favourites – with a squad including Tom Finney, Stanley Matthews, Stan Mortensen and Jackie Milburn, many back home assumed it would be a walkover. When they beat Chile 2-0 in their opening game, thanks to goals from Mortensen and Wilf Mannion, the omens were good, but what happened next proved one of the biggest shocks in the history of the game.

Thirty-three people died in the tragedy at Burnden Park in 1946.

Jackie Milburn aims one past the Spanish goalkeeper in 1950.

England, captained by Billy Wright, faced the United States in Belo Horizonte for what looked like a one-sided fixture: the Americans had only played together a few times and had little international pedigree. England dominated the first half but went behind in the 38th minute to a Joe Gaetjens goal. In the second half, the favourites became increasingly desperate in their attempts to equalise and spurned numerous chances. Many England fans, reading of the defeat in the next day's press, assumed the scoreline was a typographical error: while the result received little attention in the US, it was regarded as a sensation in the football community. A nervous England lost 1-0 to Spain in their final game and went home shell-shocked: Uruguay lifted the trophy, beating the hosts Brazil 1-0.

It has been claimed that many of the US side were of British origin, but only one, captain Ed McIlvenny, had lived or played in the country, making seven appearances for Wrexham before heading to America – nine of his team-mates were born and raised in St Louis, Missouri.

FA CUP WINNERS

1939: Portsmouth 4-1 Wolverhampton Wanderers

1940–45: No matches during Second World War

1946: Derby County 4-1 Charlton Athletic

1947: Charlton Athletic 1-0 Burnley

1948: Manchester United 4-2 Blackpool

1949: Wolverhampton Wanderers 3-1 Leicester City

1950: Arsenal 2-0 Liverpool

1951: Newcastle United 2-0 Blackpool

1952: Newcastle United 1-0 Arsenal

1953: Blackpool 4-3 Bolton Wanderers

1954: West Bromwich Albion 3-2 Preston North End

1955: Newcastle United 3-1 Manchester City

1956: Manchester City 3-1 Birmingham City

1957: Aston Villa 2-1 Manchester United

1958: Bolton Wanderers 2-0 Manchester United

1959: Nottingham Forest 2-1 Luton Town

UEFA president Gustav Wiederkehr with Jose Crahay, making the European Cup and European Cup Winners Cup draws, 1963.

1954:
UEFA Established

The French, Italian and Belgian Football Associations were the main drivers behind the formation of UEFA (Union of European Football Associations) in 1954. Africa and South America had been governed by organised bodies for decades, and a European equivalent had been a long time coming. UEFA's main purpose was to organise competitions for both countries (the European Nations Cup, first held in 1960) and clubs – the European Champions' Clubs Cup, later known as the European Cup, kicked off in 1955, but the English FA was not keen for champions Chelsea to take part. Manchester United defied the FA a year later and became the first English club to enter. Today, the European Cup has become the Champions League and

runs alongside the UEFA Cup. UEFA currently boasts 53 members, including several which lie outside Europe geographically, including Israel and Armenia.

1958:
The Munich Air Disaster

Sport often unites the nation in wonderment or expectation: on 3 February 1958, however, it brought England to its knees in despair. On that day, the most talented and charismatic squad in the country was ripped apart by tragedy, as seven players and 14 journalists, club officials and crew were killed when their flight crashed on take-off at Munich Airport. Manchester United's young 'Busby Babes' were in Germany refuelling on their return from Belgrade, where they had beaten Red Star 5-4 on aggregate in a thrilling match. Their charter plane had already failed to take off twice in the falling snow, and on the third occasion the engines failed as soon as the plane got into the air: the plane hit the runway and slid through a fence and across a road. Roger Byrne, Tommy Taylor, Eddie Colman, Mark Jones, Geoff Bent and David Pegg all died at the scene and the hugely talented Duncan Edwards died two weeks later in hospital.

Manchester was brought to a standstill as people milled the streets hopelessly when news of the disaster reached Britain. Manager Matt Busby could not speak of the events for years, although he got off his sick bed and rebuilt the club at a time when many did not see how Manchester United could even continue. Even now, it remains one of English football's blackest days.

The tangled wreckage of the airliner that crashed in Munich, decimating Matt Busby's brilliant young Manchester team.

Danny Blanchflower (1926–93)

(P: Barnsley, Aston Villa, Tottenham Hotspur, Northern Ireland; M: Northern Ireland, Chelsea)

Danny Blanchflower became the first twentieth-century captain to lift both the League and the FA Cup in the same season when he led Spurs to glory in 1961. It was a fitting achievement for the astute tactician and inspirational leader, a right-half with a superb range of passing and an excellent attitude to the game. Blanchflower only became a professional in England at the age of 23, but was soon in the Northern Ireland team and went on to play more than 330 times for Tottenham.

Tottenham Hotspur's captain Danny Blanchflower.

Today, he is best remembered for a quote which lent its title to Hunter Davies' classic book, *The Glory Game* (1972): 'The game is about glory, it's about going out and doing things with a style and a flourish, about going out and beating the other lot, not waiting for them to die of boredom.'

Sir Matt Busby (1909–94)

(P: Manchester City, Liverpool, Scotland; M: Manchester United, Scotland)

A talented and intelligent player, it was in the dugout where Sir Matt Busby made his greatest mark. He was one of the greatest managers of all time and led Manchester United to five league titles, two FA Cups and a European Cup in 16 years at Old Trafford. Busby's great strength was in building an excellent team spirit and inspiring his young players to perform beyond their years – his young charges of the mid-1950s were nicknamed the 'Busby Babes', cruelly decimated in the 1958 Munich Air Disaster. Busby was shattered by these events, but returned once more to nurture a talented crop of young players and write his name into United legend.

Famed for his intelligence and good humour but feared for his strong disciplinarian streak, he commanded respect throughout the game and inspired many to move into management themselves.

John Charles (1931–2004)

(Leeds, Juventus, Roma, Cardiff, Wales)

The most versatile player of his era, and arguably the most naturally gifted, John Charles was also the first Brit to star in Italy's Serie A. Born in Swansea, Charles

Compton first played for the Gunners in 1936 as a left winger and was named Man of the Match. He made 60 appearances for them over the next 14 years, winning the FA Cup in 1950, and became famous as the 'Brylcreem Boy' when he endorsed hair gel to a generation of football fans.

The versatile John Charles of Leeds United.

The multi-talented Arsenal player Denis Compton.

made his name at Leeds, where he is still worshipped to this day. In eight years there, he scored 150 goals, including 38 in his first year in the top flight in 1956 – a remarkable total given that he turned out in almost every outfield position during his time at Elland Road.

In 1957, he went to Juventus for a record £65,000 and led the Turin side to three titles, becoming a fans' favourite for his determined and graceful play. Homesickness took him back to Leeds, but he had another spell in Italy with Roma before ending his professional career with Cardiff.

Denis Compton (1919–97)

(Arsenal)

Denis Compton's greatest failing was simply an inability to be in two places at once. One of the few men in the twentieth century to represent England at both cricket and football, he would have excelled as a footballer had he not been quite so talented at cricket. His incredible first-class averages made him the greatest cricketer of his day, and he fitted a career with Arsenal around his other sporting commitments.

FOOTBALL WRITERS' ASSOCIATION FOOTBALLER OF THE YEAR

1948:	Stanley Matthews	Blackpool)
1949:	Johnny Carey	Manchester United
1950:	Joe Mercer	Arsenal
1951:	Harry Johnston	Blackpool
1952:	Billy Wright	Wolverhampton Wanderers
1953:	Nat Lofthouse	Bolton Wanderers
1954:	Tom Finney	Preston North End
1955:	Don Revie	Manchester City
1956:	Bert Trautmann	Manchester City
1957:	Tom Finney	Preston North End
1958:	Danny Blanchflower	Tottenham Hotspur
1959:	Syd Owen	Luton Town

Duncan Edwards (1936–58)

(Manchester United, England)

How good could Duncan Edwards have become? It is an impossible question to answer, but at the time of his death at the age of 21 the legendary wing-half had already been capped 18 times for his country. His sheer natural ability saw him first play for Manchester United at the age of 18, and their manager, Matt Busby, described him as 'the best player in the world'. Edwards died two weeks after the Munich Air Disaster, having woken from a coma to ask 'what time's kick-off on Saturday?'

Preston North End's gentleman footballer, Tom Finney.

Duncan Edwards, England and Manchester United star.

Tom Finney (b. 1922)

(Preston North End, England)

Tom Finney was not just one of his generation's most exciting players, but a true embodiment of a more gentlemanly era in football. Born across the road from Preston's Deepdale Stadium, he played his entire career for his hometown team, rejecting offers from bigger clubs every season. The decision cost him the chance to win any significant silverware, but it earned him respect throughout the game, and the nickname 'The Preston Plumber', after the extra work he took on to supplement his footballer's wage. He scored 30 goals in 76 games for England, and Bill Shankly once said: 'Tom Finney would have been great in any team, in any match and in any age – even if he had been wearing an overcoat.'

Johnny Haynes (1934–2005)

(Fulham, England)

Like Finney a one-club man, Johnny Haynes played 658 times for Fulham and was described by Pele as 'the best passer of the ball I've ever seen.' He played for England at every single age level, the first player to do so, and made 56 appearances for his country in total, 22 of them as captain. He stuck by Fulham even when they were relegated to the Second Division.

In 1961, Haynes became the first £100-a-week player, following the lifting of the maximum wage: his chairman had said he was worth that amount when the maximum wage was still in place and was therefore obliged to pay up.

Johnny Haynes (left) with England team-mate Peter Broadbent.

Tommy Lawton (1919–96)

(P: Burnley, Everton, Chelsea, Notts County, Arsenal; P&M: Brentford; M: Notts County)

Tommy Lawton had big boots to fill when he arrived at Goodison Park in 1937 as a replacement for Dixie Dean. He was an immediate success and made the England team within months, scoring 34 goals to fire Everton to the final league title before the war. The fearless striker appeared for Chelsea after the war ended, but fell out with the club and shocked football by dropping down to the Third Division to join Notts County. Naturally, he was a revelation, scoring more than 100 goals in five seasons and continuing to represent his country despite his drop in status. Lawton returned to the top flight with Arsenal in the early 1950s.

Tommy Lawton leads out the England team in 1946.

Billy Liddell (1922–2001)

(Liverpool, Scotland)

Strong, quick and with an unerring eye for goal, Billy Liddell was Liverpool's first superstar. He waited a long time for his debut, having signed before the war as a teenager; he was unable to play in the first team until the conflict ended, but made up for lost time by winning the title in his first season and went on to appear more than 500 times for the club, staying at Anfield until the age of 39. They were not the best of times for Liverpool, and the club spent the final seven seasons of his career in the Second Division, but Liddell rejected numerous suitors to stay with his first love.

Nat Lofthouse (b. 1925)

(P: Bolton, England; M: Bolton)

One of the fastest footballers of his generation, Nat Lofthouse's bravery and finishing ability were the stuff of Bolton legend. He spent his entire career in the town of his birth, with only one FA Cup winners' medal to show for his efforts. He was overlooked by his country, in part because he stayed with a relatively unfashionable team and also because he had such strong competition in England's forward

Bolton's Nat Lofthouse.

line. His England debut came aged 25, but he went on to win 33 caps and was named the 'Lion of Vienna' for his performance in a victory over Austria in 1952. After retiring, Lofthouse briefly managed Bolton and held various posts at the club for more than 20 years.

Liverpool's Billy Liddell leads out his team to play against Southend United in 1958.

Dave Mackay in his Tottenham Hotspur days.

Dave Mackay (b. 1934)

(P: Hearts, Tottenham, Derby County, Scotland;
P&M: Swindon Town; M: Nottingham Forest, Derby
County, Walsall, Doncaster Rovers, Birmingham)

Bill Nicholson rated Dave Mackay as his best-ever signing, and without the hard-as-nails Scot, Tottenham might never have achieved their magnificent double in 1961. Nicholson signed Mackay in 1959 to be the heartbeat of his team, relying on his crunching tackles and deft passing to galvanise a skilful side and turn them into winners. He was spot-on: Nicholson was a legendary hard man, both when it came to putting fear into opponents and in the way he dealt with injuries – he broke the same leg twice in nine months but made a full recovery. After Tottenham, he forged a career as a manager, guiding Derby County to an unlikely league title in 1975.

Stanley Matthews (1915–2000)

(P: Stoke City, Blackpool, England; M: Port Vale)

Stanley Matthews was the most recognisable footballer of his era, but his appeal extended beyond the game. He was an icon long before players became influential in other spheres. Recognised for his fair play and his professionalism as well as his mesmerising dribbling skills, which left the best defenders in the world trailing in his wake, he was the first footballer ever to be knighted.

Matthews spent his early career with hometown club Stoke City, but joined Blackpool in 1947, winning the FA Cup in 1953 in a match dubbed the 'Matthews Final' for the way he commanded the game. He rejoined Stoke in 1961, aged 46, and played for another four years, becoming the oldest player to appear in the First Division at the remarkable age of 50 – many believed he could have played for longer, such was his ability and fitness. He won his last England cap at 42, another record.

Stanley Matthews, playing for Blackpool in 1948.

Arsenal captain Joe Mercer clings for dear life to the FA Cup after his team's win in 1950.

Joe Mercer (1914–90)

(P: Everton, Arsenal, England; M: Sheffield United, Aston Villa, Manchester City, Coventry, England)

A powerful and determined left-back, Joe Mercer had a distinguished playing career for Everton before the war and Arsenal after it, winning five England caps in the process. He captained Arsenal to two First Division titles and an FA Cup before being forced to retire through injury. He went on to excel as a manager for his shrewd transfer judgement and popularity with players. Most notably, Mercer transformed the fortunes of Manchester City, taking them into the top flight and making them league champions within the space of two years, from 1968 to 1970.

Jackie Milburn (1924–88)

(P: Newcastle, England; M: Ipswich Town)

Jackie Milburn still watches over his beloved St James' Park: a statue of the legendary centre-forward sits at the corner of Newcastle's stadium. It is a fitting legacy for a player known simply as 'Wor Jackie' to the adoring Geordie public. Milburn signed for Newcastle while working as a miner; he attended a trial during the war with his boots wrapped in a brown paper bag. His goalscoring exploits were amazing – 200 goals in under 400 matches for Newcastle, with whom the FA Cup three times in the 1950s. Milburn was also unlucky not to play more often for England, having managed an excellent return of 10 goals from 13 appearances.

Newcastle's Jackie Milburn.

Stan Mortensen (1921–91)

(P: Blackpool, Hull, England; M: Blackpool)

Stan Mortensen holds the unique distinction of once playing in an international against his country: during a wartime match between England and Wales at a packed Wembley Stadium, a Welsh player left the field injured with his team lacking any substitutes. Mortensen was allowed to play for the opposition despite not having won a full England cap at the time; fortunately, England won 8-3. On his proper international debut, Mortensen hit four goals in a 10-0 thrashing of Portugal. He entered the record books for his hat-trick in the 1953 FA Cup final, but despite being the only player ever to record this feat the match was still known as 'The Matthews Final'.

Len Shackleton heads the ball for Sunderland.

Len Shackleton (1922–2000)

(Bradford Park Avenue, Newcastle, Sunderland, England)

A flamboyant, mischievous showman, Len Shackleton was known as 'The Clown Prince of Soccer' for his antics on and off the pitch. He loved bamboozling defenders with his remarkable skills, and his autobiography became world-famous for a chapter entitled 'The Average Director's Knowledge of Football' – it consisted of a blank page. Shackleton was also a fine inside-forward, finding the net more than 100 times in nine years with Sunderland, the club he liked to call home; he had joined the Roker Park outfit after a mediocre spell with rivals Newcastle United.

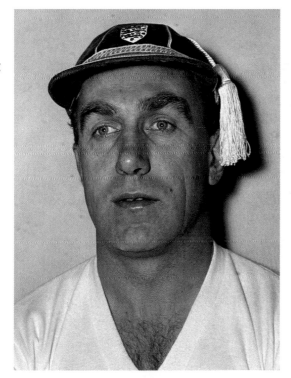

Wolverhampton Wanderers captain Billy Wright.

Billy Wright (1924–94)

(P: Wolverhampton Wanderers, England; M: Arsenal)

The first England player to win 100 caps for his country, Billy Wright was an inspirational leader and flag-bearer for Wolves' finest era. Captain of his club as they won the league three times and his country for 90 matches, 70 of them consecutive, Wright was unique in never being booked or sent off in more than 600 games for Wolves and England. He joined the club as a schoolboy apprentice and made his debut after the war; he later gained even greater celebrity by marrying Joy Beverley of chart-toppers The Beverley Sisters.

Stanley Mortensen scores Blackpool's second goal in the FA Cup Final, 2 May 1953.

Blackpool 4-3 Bolton Wanderers
FA Cup Final, Wembley, 2 May 1953

Blackpool: (Man. Joe Smith) Farm, Shimwell, Garrett, Fenton, Johnston, Robinson, Matthews, Taylor, Mortensen, Mudie, Perry

Bolton: (Man. Bill Ridding) Hanson, Ball, Banks, Wheeler, Barrass, Bell, Holden, Moir, Lofthouse, Hassall, Langton

Scorers: Blackpool: Mortensen 35, 68, 89, Perry 90; Bolton: Lofthouse 2, Moir 39, Bell 55

The 1953 FA Cup final will for ever be known as 'The Matthews Final', thanks to the incredible wing play of Stanley Matthews which enabled Blackpool to turn around a seemingly disastrous deficit and win the famous trophy for the first time in their history. However, that is a little unfair on two men who had just as big an impact on the match as Matthews: Stan Mortensen – who became

the first and only player to score a cup final hat-trick – and Bill Perry, whose last-minute winner was the final act in a fascinating end-to-end game full of skill.

Blackpool had already lost two previous post-war finals, and the omens looked poor for the Seasiders when Nat Lofthouse put Bolton ahead in less than two minutes. Blackpool looked overwhelmed in the first half, but Mortensen levelled on 39 minutes. Wanderers went 3-1 up before the hour and the game seemed as good as over,

Alf Ramsey shoots one past Hungarian goalkeeper Gyula Grosics.

but Matthews went into overdrive, forcing the defence to retreat. He set up two more for Mortensen to level the scores with a minute left, and then sent the ball across the face of the box for Perry to leave Bolton stunned.

England 3-6 Hungary
Friendly International, Wembley, 25 November 1953

England: (Man. Walter Winterbottom) Merrick, Ramsey, Eckersley, Wright, Johnston, Dickinson, Matthews, Taylor, Mortensen, Sewell, Robb

Hungary: (Man. Gustav Sebes) Grosics (Geller), Buzansky, Lantos, Bozsik, Lorant, Zakarias, Budai, Kocsis, Hidegkuti, Puskas, Czibor

Scorers: England: Sewell 13, Mortensen 38, Ramsey 57; Hungary: Hidegkuti 1, 20, 53, Puskas 24, 27, Boszik 50

England had never lost to a team from outside the British Isles, but all that was to change dramatically in 1953, in a friendly match which changed the course of the nation's football destiny. Hungary were Olympic champions and were gaining a fearsome reputation: the game had been eagerly anticipated, but England were still expected to win. What happened was a demolition – England were far from terrible, but their opponents' tactical awareness and ball skills meant they were chasing shadows for much of the match. One of Hungary's masterstrokes was to play Nandor Hidegkuti, one of their most gifted players, just behind the strikers, giving him licence to roam around the pitch.

Hidegkuti's marker never knew where he was going next, which left huge gaps for other players to exploit. Hidegkuti opened the scoring within just 90 seconds and went on to fire a hat-trick; the legendary Ferenc Puskas scored two, the first of which saw him drag the ball back sublimely to outfox Billy Wright. The result was a sensation, and Hungary won the return in Budapest 7-1 to prove it was no fluke. It woke English fans, players and managers up to the fact that foreigners were finding new and better ways to play the game, and forced them to adopt methods from abroad in their own training and planning.

Manchester City 3-1 Birmingham City
FA Cup Final, Wembley, 5 May 1956

Manchester City: (Man. Les McDowall) Trautmann, Leivers, Little, Barnes, Ewing, Paul, Johnstone, Hayes, Revie, Dyson, Clarke

Birmingham: (Man. Arthur Turner) Merrick, Hall, Green, Newman, Smith, Boyd, Astall, Kinsey, Brown, Murphy, Govan

Scorers: Man City: Hayes 3, Dyson 65, Johnstone 68; Birmingham: Kinsey 15

The 1956 FA Cup final was a classic match in its own right, but is best remembered for one particularly famous incident: with 15 minutes left on the clock and his team leading 3-1, Manchester City's German goalkeeper Bert Trautmann dived at the feet of an onrushing forward and collided, collapsing in agony. He bravely played on, and X-rays revealed he had broken his neck: Prince Phillip asked him, when presenting his winner's medal, why he was holding his neck in such a strange position.

The match was the pinnacle of Trautmann's remarkable career – a former Luftwaffe pilot and prisoner of war, City fans threatened to boycott the club when he signed in 1949, but his brilliance between the posts soon won them over and he played more than 500 matches, becoming the club's greatest custodian in the process.

FOOTBALL LEAGUE CHAMPIONS

1939–46:	League abandoned due to Second World War
1946/47:	Liverpool
1947/48:	Arsenal
1948/49:	Portsmouth
1949/50:	Portsmouth
1950/51:	Tottenham Hotspur
1951/52:	Manchester United
1952/53:	Arsenal
1953/54:	Wolverhampton Wanderers
1954/55:	Chelsea
1955/56:	Manchester United
1956/57:	Manchester United
1957/58:	Wolverhampton Wanderers
1958/59:	Wolverhampton Wanderers
1959/60:	Burnley

Manchester United, 1952–58
Matt Busby

Key Players: Duncan Edwards (wing-half), Jackie Blanchflower (centre-half), Roger Byrne (full-back)

Trophies: Football League 1952, 1956, 1957

The young Manchester United team of the 1950s were arguably the finest group of British talent ever assembled in a club side, which makes it all the more poignant that they were ripped apart by tragedy before they reached the height of their powers. Had the Munich Air Disaster not taken place in 1958, it might have been Duncan Edwards lifting the World Cup for England in 1966, joined by several Manchester United team-mates, and the club might have won the double of League and FA Cup before Tottenham did in 1961.

The Busby Babes
As it was, the 'Busby Babes' – named after Matt Busby, the forward-thinking manager who moulded them – were the outstanding team of their era, always entertaining and packed with individual talent. Throughout his career, Busby disliked paying transfer fees and preferred to put the emphasis on youth. When he arrived at Old Trafford in 1945, he put a system in place for spotting and developing outstanding schoolboys, and when several of the side who landed the 1952 title began to need replacing, Busby drew new blood from the youth team ranks. Edwards was a prodigious talent and a great team player, while Jackie Blanchflower was intelligent and hard-working. Roger Byrne was promoted to captain and Dennis Viollet led the team from the front. Bobby Charlton came on the scene in 1956 and immediately looked the most capable of them all, a direct and unselfish striker with a blistering shot.

Tragedy Strikes
Two more titles followed, in 1956 and 1957, and Europe soon beckoned. There was every possibility that the club could win the double and the European Cup in 1958, but events in Munich ended all that in the cruellest way imaginable. Seven players were killed instantly, and Edwards

Matt Busby with his 'Babes': Albert Scanlon, Colin Webster, John Doherty, Tony Hawesworth, Alec Dawson and Paddy Kennedy.

died two weeks later. Blanchflower would never play again and Busby himself was hospitalised for two months. He was back at work as soon as possible, and although the club could only finish ninth in the league with what was essentially a reserve team, they did reach the cup final, losing 2-0 to Bolton on a highly emotional occasion.

The Red Devils

Busby encouraged the club to adopt a new 'Red Devils' nickname in the 1960s, partly to erase the memories of the events in Munich and enable United to move on and prepare themselves for a new era of achievement, which culminated in another crop of homegrown talent winning the 1968 European Cup.

Wolves, 1954–60
Stan Cullis

Key Players: Billy Wright (centre-half), Ron Flowers (inside-forward), Jimmy Mullen (winger)

Trophies: Football League 1954, 1958, 1959; FA Cup 1960

Eyebrows were raised among Wolverhampton Wanderers fans when Stan Cullis was appointed as their new manager in 1948. He had been an inspirational player for the club before and during the war, but many questioned whether someone so inexperienced could bring glory to a club which had never lived up to expectations. But Cullis proved the doubters wrong in spectacular style.

An United Squad

In his first season, he landed the FA Cup, and in 1954 Wolves were champions for the first time in their history, seeing off West Midlands rivals West Bromwich Albion in the process. Cullis built his team around the inspirational figure of Billy Wright, but it was the unity of the squad which was Wolves' greatest asset; the manager worked hard at forging this, and at building an attractive, passing style which tore the heart out of opponents. Wolves went on to win the league again in 1958 and 1959, and a year later they were hopeful of making it three in a row – however, they lost out to Burnley on the final day of the season and had to be content with beating Blackburn 3-0 to land the FA Cup.

Under The Floodlights

Arguably Wolves' greatest achievements in this era, however, were the floodlit friendlies which drew huge crowds to Molineux and played an indirect part in bringing about the European Cup. The club invited teams from Austria, Russia, Argentina and Israel to play midweek games under the ground's new floodlights, and all were dispatched by Cullis' men. The sternest test arrived in December 1954 when, on a chilly night in Wolverhampton, the great Honved team arrived. Honved had provided the nucleus of the Hungarian team which had beaten England the previous year. In front of 55,000, Sandor Kocsis and Ferenc Machos put the visitors 2-0 up, with Ferenc Puskas pulling the strings. However, Cullis sent his team out determined to take the game to their opponents in the second half, and two goals from Walter Swinbourne, plus a Johnny Hancocks penalty, sent the crowd home delighted. The next day's *Daily Mail* claimed 'Wolves are champions of the world now' and Cullis certainly agreed – the challenges he issued to the rest of Europe helped start the ball rolling towards a European Cup, but by the time it arrived Wolves and their manager were in no position to repeat their triumphs of the 1950s.

The Wolverhampton Wanderers team that won the FA Cup in 1960. Manager Stan Cullis sits with the Cup.

The Second World War

The final matches of peacetime took place on Saturday 2 September 1939; it was only the second weekend of the 1939/40 season, but the international situation was already serious enough that most grounds were only half-full. War was declared the next day, and an emergency law banning large crowds meant that football at all levels had to be suspended immediately.

Joining The War Effort

Many professional players had been enlisting in the army for some time. The playing personnel of Liverpool, West Ham and Bolton had all signed up en masse to the Territorials, for example (many of the Bolton players were involved in the evacuation of Dunkirk), and hundreds of players from every club in Britain joined the war effort. While some fought on the frontline, others joined the police and fire services at home – Leslie Compton, brother of Denis and himself an Arsenal and England stalwart, was a member of the fire brigade for the duration of the conflict. Many players enrolled on the Army Physical Training course, including Joe Mercer and Walter Winterbottom, and they helped drill young recruits and improve their standards of fitness.

Members of the armed forces queue for half-price tickets, 1943.

All Change

Regional matches soon started taking place, with a number of regional championships and cups competed for during the war, but they were haphazard affairs: all matches required the permission of the police and the Home Office, and were subject to change at short notice if it was feared they might be a target for a German attack. Because of this, points averages rather than points totals were used to separate sides – which is how Manchester United were 1942 national champions despite gaining three points less than Blackpool. Players generally

Brothers Leslie (left) and Denis Compton.

appeared for the team nearest where they were stationed, and for those men who were moved around the country, this meant they could end up 'guesting' for dozens of clubs. England international Tommy Lawton, for example, played for several Scottish sides as well as Everton (the club he was contracted to), Tranmere Rovers and Aldershot, who became one of the most popular teams during the war due to the large RAF base in the town. Around 25 internationals turned out for the Hampshire side during the war, including Blackburn's Arthur Cunliffe and England goalkeeper Frank Swift. Many teenagers too young to go to war were given premature top-flight debuts during this period.

Volunteers tidy up a football pitch in London after a bomb was dropped on it during an air raid.

Aiding Morale

A number of wartime internationals were also played between the Home Nations, but these are counted as unofficial matches. Many well-known grounds were hit by the Luftwaffe: Arsenal's North Bank roof was struck and in March 1941, Old Trafford's pitch was hit and the main stand destroyed, which meant Manchester United had to share with bitter rivals Manchester City even after the war was over. Swindon and Preston both saw their grounds used as prisoner of war camps. Around 80 professionals were killed in combat, including Arsenal stars Leslie Jack and Cyril Tooze and United's Hubert Redwood. Football emerged from the war with its reputation enhanced: it was widely acknowledged that by giving people entertainment and hope during the years of conflict, it had aided morale back home.

Post-War Football

Although Germany's surrender in May 1945 meant there was technically enough time to start the 1945/46 season, in reality the English game was in disarray at this point.

Finding Their Feet

Many of the stars of the pre-war era had been killed or injured or were now too old to compete at the highest level, and clubs had not been able to develop youth systems and find new young players to replace them during the chaos of the war years. Several grounds, including Old Trafford, were unfit for use, so the 1945/46 campaign was still a regional affair decided on points averages. It was kept deliberately low-key, but when football returned properly in August 1946 it was to spectacular effect: almost every club experienced sell-out crowds as spectators flocked back to see what they had been missing. They

were rewarded with a thrilling title race, Liverpool pipping Manchester United by a single point, and they kept coming back over the coming seasons.

A Golden Age

The 1948/49 season was the best-attended in English history, with a total of 41,244,295 fans turning up over the course of the season, equating to an average of more than a million per weekend. The nine seasons immediately

England coach and manager Walter Winterbottom.

following the war were nine of the 10 best supported in the history of the English professional game. A drop in average entry prices following the war had some effect on these figures, and later sharp rises in prices (up to two shillings and sixpence for a First Division game in 1960) saw equally sharp declines in attendances, as football began to compete with other leisure pursuits. Still, those post-war years were a golden age for English football – and a colourful one, too, as crowds adorned by scarves and ribbons, many carrying rattles, created a carnival atmosphere inside grounds.

Above: An expectant crowd watches Wolves v. Leicester City, 1949.
Left: England beats Germany in their first game since the war.

1960-69

The 1960s was a triumphant era for English football, both on and off the pitch. The finest generation of English talent ever seen had been assembled by national team manager Alf Ramsey, and Matt Busby was working similar miracles with a post-Munich Manchester United at Old Trafford.

The abolition of the maximum wage was just the first step in the commercialisation of the game, and by the end of the decade, the biggest names were earning more from endorsements and other commercial enterprises than they were from playing football. The defining player of the 1960s, however, was not English: George Best was part pop-star, part sublimely gifted footballer, at the heart of everything Busby's team achieved and the first player to enter the national consciousness to such a degree that he was widely recognised even by those who knew nothing about the game. United lifted the European Cup in 1968, becoming the first English club to do so, and Best was assured his place in history.

Two years earlier, Ramsey's England had won the World Cup at Wembley, the defining victory in English football history and the starting point for a new wave of interest in football across the country.

EVENTS

1960/61:
Inaugural League Cup Season

English football's 'third competition' was the brainchild of Football League secretary Alan Hardaker, who saw it as a way of giving smaller clubs an extra chance of a money-spinning draw against a bigger team. The matches were to be played over two legs and every Football League club was to enter, but the first season was marred when five leading clubs – Arsenal, Sheffield Wednesday, Tottenham, West Bromwich and Wolves – refused to take part because they did not see the point in adding to their already-busy fixture lists.

It took some time for the competition to gain popularity (Manchester United entered in 1960, but did not take part again until 1966, for instance) and it was not until a European place was guaranteed for the winners later in the decade that every major club signed up. The absence of some of the big guns in the early years helped make the League Cup a popular competition for the underdogs: Second Division Rotherham United reached the first final, losing 3-2 on aggregate to Aston Villa, while in 1962 Fourth Division Rochdale lost out in the final to Norwich City.

Today, the competition is known as the Carling Cup, and has survived despite falling attendances to become a showcase for larger clubs' young talent.

The Rangers and Fiorentina captains exchange pennants at the start of a match in 1961.

1961:
Maximum Wage Abolished

Fulham player and noted innovator Jimmy Hill became chairman of the Professional Footballers' Association in 1957 and immediately began campaigning to scrap the minimum wage, which was restricting players' earnings to £20 per week. The ruling had been in place for 60 years. A number of leading stars, such as John Charles

PFA chairman Jimmy Hill reviews the meeting minutes before a group of journalists.

and Jimmy Greaves, were beginning to go abroad in search of better conditions, and Hill and other PFA campaigners believed it was unfair that English football was the only industry in the developed world subject to such restrictions.

Talks between the PFA, Football League and key government figures did not get very far, and in 1961 Hill threatened to call a strike among professionals which would lead to the cancellation of the entire Football League programme. The authorities backed down and immediately abolished the maximum wage. Hill's Fulham team-mate Johnny Haynes was the first man to benefit, seeing his weekly pay shoot up to £100 per week overnight, although other players' earnings did not rise by much at first – the double-winning Arsenal team of 1971 were on an average of £55 per week each.

FA CUP WINNERS

1960:	Wolverhampton Wanderers 3-0 Blackburn Rovers
1961:	Tottenham Hotspur 2-0 Leicester City
1962:	Tottenham Hotspur 3-1 Burnley
1963:	Manchester United 3-1 Leicester City
1964:	West Ham United 3-2 Preston North End
1965:	Liverpool 2-1 Leeds United
1966:	Everton 3-2 Sheffield Wednesday
1967:	Tottenham Hotspur 2-1 Chelsea
1968:	West Bromwich Albion 1-0 Everton
1969:	Manchester City 1-0 Leicester City

1964:
First *Match Of The Day* Airs

Kenneth Wolstenholme was at the helm for the first outing of a football institution: the BBC's *Match Of The Day* hit the airwaves on Saturday 22 August 1964, the opening day of the season. The new highlights show had chosen Liverpool v Arsenal at Anfield as its first featured game, but only 20,000 viewers tuned in to see the match. It was not until the World Cup win in 1966 took football to a wider audience that *Match Of The Day* really cemented its place in the television schedules: two years after its debut, the programme was attracting five million viewers: 'I will explain some of the more technical points of the game as we go along,' Wolstenholme promised in the 1966 season.

By 1972, the programme was being watched in colour by 12 million, and John Motson was getting over-excited as Hereford knocked Newcastle out of the FA Cup. Jimmy Hill

took over as presenter a year later and became the most public face of the show. *Match Of The Day* was barely screened between 1985 and 1992, but the birth of the Premier League led to the BBC sharing television rights with Sky and the return of the popular highlights show, fronted by Des Lynam, and later former England international Gary Lineker.

1968:
Manchester United Win European Cup

Celtic had become the first British club to win Europe's newest competition in 1967, but a year later Manchester United followed suit in remarkable style. Matt Busby's team had failed to win a match, or even score a single goal, away from home as they reached the semi-finals by beating Hibernians of Malta, FK Sarajevo and

Liverpool's Gordon Wallace scores the team's second goal against Arsenal in the first game televised on *Match of the Day*.

Matt Busby, flanked by Pat Crerand and George Best, after Manchester United win the European Cup, 30 May 1968.

Gornik Zabrze of Poland, and when they went 3-1 down in Madrid in the second leg of the semi-final against Real they looked down and out. Fortunately, David Sadler levelled the tie on aggregate (United had won the first leg 1-0 at Old Trafford) and Bill Foulkes sent them through to meet Benfica. Extra time was needed, thanks to Alex Stepney's penalty save which kept United in the game,

but two goals from Bobby Charlton and one apiece from George Best and Brian Kidd set up a 4-1 victory.

It was a result which had been coming for some time: United had been getting closer to the trophy each year since they demolished Benfica 5-1 at the Stadium of Light in 1965 but came unstuck against Partizan Belgrade when it seemed certain they would reach the final that year.

PLERS

PLAYERS

Alan Ball (b. 1945)

(P: Blackpool, Everton, Arsenal, Southampton, Bristol Rovers, England; M: Blackpool, Portsmouth, Stoke, Exeter, Southampton, Manchester City)

A pint-sized terrier in midfield with an incredible work-rate, Alan Ball was the youngest of England's 1966 World Cup winners, aged 20, and an unsung hero of the final. He had made his debut the previous season as a teenager, and went on to play 72 times for his country, although he lost his captaincy and was dropped from the England squad when Don Revie became manager in 1976, and never appeared again. As a manager, he achieved some success with Portsmouth and Exeter but was unable to win over the Manchester City supporters and retired from coaching aged 54.

Gordon Banks (b. 1937)

(Chesterfield, Leicester City, Stoke, England)

One of the heroes of England's World Cup win, Gordon Banks – or 'Banks of England' as he was dubbed by the press – is widely regarded as one of the best goalkeepers the world has ever seen. If his exploits in 1966 were not enough, his incredible one-handed save from a Pele header in the 1970 World Cup finals was arguably the most spectacular stop of all time. Banks played 73 times for the national team, and made more than 400 top-flight appearances for Leicester and Stoke before a car crash in 1972 robbed him of the sight in one eye. He went on to become one of the first high-profile players in the North American Soccer League (NASL).

Leicester City and England goalkeeper Gordon Banks.

George Best (1946–2005)

(Manchester United, Stockport County, Fulham, Hibernian, Bournemouth, Northern Ireland)

Quite simply the greatest footballer these islands ever produced, and the only one who could rival Pele and Diego Maradona for the title of world's best player, the reaction across Britain to George Best's death in 2005 showed the affection he was held in by football fans everywhere.

Belfast-born Best was spotted as a 15-year-old by Manchester United scout Bob Bishop, who sent manager Matt Busby a telegram reading 'I have found a genius.' Best was small and slight, but the ball seemed glued to his foot (he could use either equally effectively) and he had an unerring eye for goal for a winger. His dazzling form in the 1968 European Cup final sealed his legend, having already landed the league title twice. He became a superstar off the pitch for his looks and easy demeanour, endorsing products and living the high life, but alcoholism was beginning to take its toll and in 1974 Best and United parted ways for good.

Alan Ball takes a throw-in.

Manchester United's flawed hero George Best.

He spent the next nine years as a nomad, appearing in Scotland, Stockport and the US while enjoying a brief Indian summer with Fulham, but despite the efforts of team-mates and other football luminaries, Best could never win his battle with the bottle.

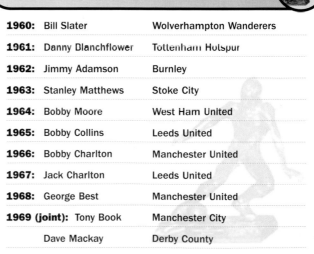

FOOTBALL WRITERS' ASSOCIATION FOOTBALLER OF THE YEAR

1960:	Bill Slater	Wolverhampton Wanderers
1961:	Danny Blanchflower	Tottenham Hotspur
1962:	Jimmy Adamson	Burnley
1963:	Stanley Matthews	Stoke City
1964:	Bobby Moore	West Ham United
1965:	Bobby Collins	Leeds United
1966:	Bobby Charlton	Manchester United
1967:	Jack Charlton	Leeds United
1968:	George Best	Manchester United
1969 (joint):	Tony Book	Manchester City
	Dave Mackay	Derby County

Bobby Charlton (b. 1937)

(Manchester United, Preston, England)

Bobby Charlton survived the Munich Air Disaster to become the fulcrum of Manchester United's success in the 1960s and one of the key figures in England's World Cup win. The clean-cut antithesis to George Best's excesses, Charlton was nonetheless a skilful and intelligent forward (generally playing just behind the strikers) who inspired respect among team-mates and opponents, and became one of English football's finest ambassadors. He made his United debut in 1956 and was soon a first-team regular, making his England bow in 1958, soon after

Bobby Charlton smiles for England, 1966.

Munich, although he did not appear in that year's World Cup. By 1966, he was widely regarded as England's finest individual, and his two goals in the semi-final with Portugal put England into the final. In all, he scored 49 times to become his country's greatest-ever goalscorer.

Jack Charlton (b. 1935)

(P: Leeds, England; M: Middlesbrough, Sheffield Wednesday, Newcastle, Republic of Ireland)

Elder brother of Bobby and a fine player in his own right, Jack Charlton was an even higher-profile manager than he was a player. The gangly centre-back might have been inelegant but he was effective, spending 21 years at Leeds United and finally being rewarded with the league title in 1969, having seen the club rise from the lower divisions to the top flight. Charlton only made his England debut at the age of 30, 12 months before the World Cup finals, but he cemented his place with a series of no-nonsense performances and was a rock in the final itself.

After retiring from the game and tasting managerial success with Middlesbrough and Sheffield Wednesday, he took over the vacant Republic of Ireland post and steered the unfancied team to success in two World Cups, in 1990 and 1994, defeating Italy in the latter tournament to make the group phase and only going out of the former to the Italians in the quarter-finals.

Tommy Docherty (b. 1928)

(P: Celtic, Preston, Arsenal, Chelsea, Scotland; M: Chelsea, Rotherham, QPR, Aston Villa, Porto, Hull, Manchester United, Derby, Preston, Wolves, Scotland)

A controversial manager who was at the helm of many leading clubs during a 25-year career in the dugout, Tommy Docherty's often brash statements delighted the press and fans but did not keep him in any one position for long. After a long career with Preston which included 25 Scotland caps, the Glaswegian took over at Chelsea, nurturing many fine young players but failing to bring silverware. He spent no more than a few months in any

job, but his abilities in spotting and motivating players made him a sought-after manager, and in 1972 he embarked on five colourful seasons at Manchester United, stabilising a club on a downward spiral before being sacked for conducting an affair with the physio's wife.

Johnny Giles (b. 1940)

(P: Manchester United, Leeds, Republic of Ireland; P&M: West Brom)

Johnny Giles was thrown into the Manchester United first team in the

Johnny Giles.

wake of the Munich Disaster and held a place for several seasons, winning the 1963 FA Cup, before seeking regular football elsewhere. He joined Leeds and forged a fruitful central midfield partnership with Billy Bremner which made the team one of the most feared in the First Division and landed them the 1969 and 1974 titles, the 1972 FA Cup and two Fairs Cups (the equivalent of the UEFA Cup) during a 12-year career. Giles later combined a player-manager role with West Brom with the same job for his country, but left management to become a broadcaster in Ireland.

Jimmy Greaves (b. 1940)

(Chelsea, AC Milan, Tottenham, West Ham, England)

Spurs star Jimmy Greaves.

Few strikers in history have scored at the rate Jimmy Greaves managed for club and country: 357 in 516 First Division matches and 44 in 57 for England. An injury in the group matches in 1966 meant he was confined to the stands as England won the World Cup, a major disappointment in his career. He first caught the eye at Chelsea, scoring 41 times in the 1960/61 season alone to earn a move to Italian giants AC Milan. Greaves failed to settle in Serie A and was back after 12 games, spending nine seasons at Tottenham and becoming a White Hart Lane legend under Bill Nicholson. On retirement, he fought alcoholism and became a successful broadcaster.

Jimmy Hill (b. 1928)

(P: Brentford, Fulham; M: Coventry)

The first person ever to be a player, manager, coach, director and chairman of a Football League club, Jimmy Hill has a unique place in the nation's affections and introduced many innovations to the game. After a long career with Fulham, during which he had been instrumental in abolishing the maximum wage and changing the transfer system, Hill managed Coventry and later became chairman, building the first all-seater football ground and coming up with many novel ideas to bring in the crowds, including fireworks and free tickets for children. He later persuaded the FA to adopt three points for a win and became a notable broadcaster as host of *Match Of The Day* and other football programmes.

Roger Hunt (b. 1938)

(Liverpool, Bolton, England)

Roger Hunt.

The 'other' striker in England's World Cup final win, Roger Hunt's unselfish work and immediate understanding with Geoff Hurst was crucial in 1966. Hunt scored 285 goals in 10 years at Liverpool to become one of the Anfield club's deadliest strikers of all time. He scored on his England debut against Austria in 1962 and hit 18 in 34 appearances for his country – he was unfortunate that he played in an era when England boasted so many fine strikers, as he might otherwise have won twice as many caps.

Geoff Hurst (b. 1941)

(P: West Ham, Stoke, West Brom, England; M: Chelsea)

When the 1966 World Cup came around, Geoff Hurst had played only eight times for England and was playing second fiddle to Roger Hunt and Jimmy Greaves in Alf Ramsey's pecking order. Yet when Greaves was injured in the final group game with France, Hurst stepped into the limelight and scored the winner to beat Argentina 1-0 in an ill-tempered quarter-final. He retained his place on merit and famously wrote his name into the record books as the only man ever to score a hat-trick in a World Cup final. Hurst left the game in the 1970s after a brief spell as manager of Chelsea, but had sealed his position as an England legend.

Record-breaker Geoff Hurst – the only man ever to score a hat-trick in a World Cup final.

Denis Law (b. 1940)

(Huddersfield Town, Manchester City, Torino, Manchester United, Scotland)

Considered by many to be Manchester United's finest-ever striker, Denis Law was in fact a legend on both sides of the city. He first rose to prominence when he scored 23 times in 50 matches for Manchester City, earning a move to Torino of Italy in 1961. The transfer proved short-lived, and Matt Busby chose Law as the goalpoacher to fire his Manchester United side to glory. Law won the league twice with United and scored 171 league goals for them, but was injured for the 1968 European Cup final. He was devastated in 1974 when his goal for City relegated United on the final day of the season.

Manchester United's Denis Law.

Bobby Moore (1941–93)

(P: West Ham, Fulham, England; M: Oxford, Southend United)

An inspirational skipper and a fine sportsman, Bobby Moore was the public face of English sport for decades, lifting the World Cup to crown a career of achievement at the highest level of the game. Moore was not just a leader: he was also the best centre-half of his generation, as his monumental battle with Pele (who considered him his worthiest adversary) in 1970 showed. He won 108 caps in all for his country and played 544 times for his beloved West Ham. He struggled to move on when he left the game in 1977, and many felt he was shunned by the Football Association when he should have been used as an ambassador for English football.

players and brought the club the 1961 double: his favoured pass-and-move game was pretty to watch and devastatingly effective. After retiring in 1974, he continued to live around the corner from the Spurs ground and was a director of the club until his death.

Martin Peters (b. 1943)

(P: West Ham, Tottenham, Norwich, Sheffield United, England; M: Sheffield United)

Martin Peters' goal for England in the 1966 World Cup final marked a rapid rise to fame for a player who the previous season had been unable to hold down a regular place for West Ham. Super-fit and intelligent, Peters was described by club manager Ron Greenwood as being '10 years ahead of his time' for the thoughtful way in which he played. Once he arrived in the England team in May 1966, a month before the World Cup began, he kept his place for seven years, winning 67 caps in all and excelling for Spurs when he later left Upton Park.

England and West Ham United captain Bobby Moore.

Bill Nicholson (1919–2004)

(P: Tottenham, England; M: Tottenham)

Although he was born and raised in Yorkshire, Bill Nicholson devoted his life to Tottenham Hotspur. He spent 17 seasons with the club as a player and also won one England cap, scoring on his debut but losing his place to Billy Wright in the next match. When he was appointed manager in 1958 he set about transforming the White Hart Lane outfit – in fact, they won 10-4 in his first match. Nicholson's coaching skills and quiet confidence inspired his

Moore's team-mate Martin Peters.

Alf Ramsey (1920–99)

(P: Southampton, Tottenham, England;

M: Ipswich Town, England)

There were more flamboyant managers than Alf Ramsey, but few more effective, and his skill in blending different types of players into a cohesive unit under intense pressure in 1966 marks him out as one of the all-time greats. After a distinguished playing career which included 32 caps, Ramsey saw Ipswich promoted twice and won the First Division in 1963 in one of the unlikeliest title victories ever. He was an obvious choice for England soon afterwards and brought in a number of young players he believed could shake up the set-up. Ramsey continued with England through a testing 1970 World Cup campaign but left in 1974 and did not manage again.

Alf Ramsey ponders his chances of success in the 1966 World Cup.

Legendary player and manager Bill Shankly.

Bill Shankly (1913–81)

(P: Carlisle, Preston, Scotland; M: Carlisle, Grimsby, Workington, Huddersfield, Liverpool)

Bill Shankly took the values of the tough Ayrshire mining village where he was raised and used them to forge a career as one of the greatest managers in the English game. A fierce motivator and feared tactician, Shankly also came out with some of the game's most memorable one-liners – including 'football's not a matter of life or death … it's more important than that', which is frequently taken out of context. Appointed in 1959, he built teams in his own image – rugged and steely but also entertaining – and in 15 years at Anfield won three First Divisions, two FA Cups and the UEFA Cup. The Shankly legacy left a system in place which successive managers used to steer Liverpool to glory for decades to come.

Nobby Stiles (b. 1942)

(P: Manchester United, Middlesbrough, Preston, England; M: Preston, West Brom)

Though he is one of the least-discussed members of the 1966 team, Nobby Stiles' contribution was vital. Having established himself as a Manchester United regular, Alf Ramsey tried him out as a ball-winning midfielder in the national team in 1965 and liked what he saw: Stiles'

tenacious tackling and never-say-die attitude became vital to the team. He played for United until 1971 and won 28 caps in total, but most fans' abiding memory will be Stiles dancing with the World Cup on the Wembley pitch.

Nobby Stiles – another 1966 World Cup veteran.

MATCHES

England 4-2 West Germany

World Cup Final, Wembley, 30 July 1966

England: (Man. Alf Ramsey) Banks, Cohen, Wilson, Stiles, J. Charlton, Moore, Ball, Hunt, R. Charlton, Hurst, Peters

West Germany: (Man. Helmut Schön) Tikowski, Hottges, Schnellinger, Beckenbauer, Shulz, Weber, Haller, Overath, Seeler, Held, Emmerich

Scorers: England: Hurst 19, 98, 120, Peters 78; West Germany: Haller 12, Weber 90

Wolfgang Weber equalises for West Germany during the World Cup final in England, 1966.

The 1966 World Cup final was not only England's finest hour – it was also an excellent end-to-end game of football with a moment of controversy and plenty of twists and turns. Alf Ramsey was careful to keep his players calm and collected before the match, but they made a disastrous start when Germany took the lead in just 12 minutes. A scrappy Geoff Hurst goal seven minutes later put England level and helped them gradually assert themselves on the game. Both teams created chances, but on 78 minutes, Martin Peters' smart finish put the hosts back in control and victory was within sight.

In the last minute, Jack Charlton gave away a free-kick England were never able to clear and Wolfgang Weber finished to force extra time. The England players looked shaken, but their opponents never took the opportunity to capitalise; eight minutes into extra time, Geoff Hurst's shot cannoned off the crossbar and down onto the goal-line. After the referee consulted with his Russian linesman, the goal was awarded. Germany tried to press their way back into the match but began to leave bigger gaps at the back, and in the final minute Hurst lashed the ball home to make the game safe, accompanied by Kenneth Wolstenholme's famous commentary: '...some people are on the pitch ... they think it's all over. It is now!'

Man U's David Sadler celebrates their European Cup win.

Manchester United 4-1 Benfica

European Cup Final, Wembley, 29 May 1968

Manchester United: (Man. Matt Busby) Stepney, Dunne, Foulkes, Stiles, Brennan, Sadler, Crerand, Charlton, Best, Kidd, Aston

Benfica: (Man. Otto Gloria) Henrique, Adolfo, Cruz, Graca, Humberto, Jacinto, Augusto, Eusebio, Torres, Coluna, Simones

Scorers: Manchester United: Charlton 53, 99, Best 93, Kidd 94; Benfica: Graca 75

Ten years after the devastation of Munich, Manchester United's finest hour came at Wembley. For Matt Busby, it was the realisation of a dream,

FOOTBALL LEAGUE CHAMPIONS

1960/61:	Tottenham Hotspur
1961/62:	Ipswich Town
1962/63:	Everton
1963/64:	Liverpool
1964/65:	Manchester United
1965/66:	Liverpool
1966/67:	Manchester United
1967/68:	Manchester City
1968/69:	Leeds United
1969/70:	Everton

to become the first English team to lift the European Cup. It was also a night when two very different stars shone for United – the virtuoso talents of George Best, who Benfica failed to mark out of the game, and the perfect timing and finishing skills of Bobby Charlton. In a tense first 90 minutes, Charlton put United ahead when he headed home in the second half. United had the chances to make the game safe but failed to take them, and on 75 minutes Graca equalised for Benfica.

An exhausted United then let the great Eusebio through on goal, and only a classic save from Alex Stepney kept Busby's team in the game. Best started the comeback, rounding defenders and keeper in style to put United ahead, before Brian Kidd notched a goal on his 19th birthday and Charlton scored again to seal victory. It was an emotional night, tinged by sadness, but one of the great European matches for English teams and a proud moment for United.

TEAMS

Tottenham Hotspur, 1960–61
Bill Nicholson

Key Players: Dave Mackay (centre-half), Danny Blanchflower (right-half), Cliff Jones (winger)

Trophies: Football League 1961, FA Cup 1961

Many regard the Tottenham team of 1960–61 as the finest English club side of the twentieth century: certainly they were the first that century to win the famed double of League and FA Cup in the same season, but they were unable to repeat their feat or to stamp their authority across the 1960s as they might have hoped.

Clever Tactics

The seeds of the double were sewn with the appointment in 1958 of Bill Nicholson as Spurs manager; young, ambitious and tactically aware, Nicholson did not change the personnel of a failing Tottenham team significantly but he did change the way they played, bringing in a 'push and run' system which meant players were immediately looking to pass the ball to a team-mate. When a player received the ball, he would lay it off as quickly as possible and then move into a new position to keep the opposition on their toes and look for the next pass. This intricate system of passing needed skilled technical players, which Nicholson had in abundance, but he still had to curb their natural inclinations to take players on and dribble excessively with the ball.

Spurs On Fire

By 1960, his work was done and Spurs were ready to begin their ascent. Nicholson also dropped out-of-form veteran captain Danny Blanchflower in 1959, encouraging the player to fit into the new mentality and become the architect of a new system on the pitch: by the time Blanchflower was reinstated, he was like a new player. Tottenham started with a flourish: they won their first 11 league games on the bounce and went 16 unbeaten. Bobby Smith was on fire up front, and would score 28 league goals in his finest season in a Tottenham shirt. Cliff Jones supplied a constant stream of ammunition for the forward line, and Dave Mackay terrified the opposition with his steely displays.

Winning The Double

When second-placed Sheffield Wednesday visited White Hart Lane in April, it was their last chance to halt the Spurs juggernaut: they lost 2-1 thanks to Les Allen's winner and the championship was sealed. Spurs faced Leicester City in the FA Cup final, but it seemed the curse which had seen several previous league champions mess up their chance of a double was about to strike again: even with a man injured and unable to play any active part in the game from the 15th minute onwards, Leicester made life hard and hung on until the 69th minute, when Smith – who had sneaked out of the team hotel for pain-killing injections without telling Nicholson – stole in to break the deadlock. Allen added a second, and half of north London partied into the night.

Spurs captain Danny Blanchflower holds aloft the FA Cup, carried by his team-mates, on 6 May 1961. This team was widely regarded as the finest of the era.

FOOTBALL LEAGUE CUP WINNERS

1961:	Aston Villa 3-2 Rotherham United
1962:	Norwich City 4-0 Rochdale
1963:	Birmingham City 3-1 Aston Villa
1964:	Leicester City 4-3 Stoke City
1965:	Chelsea 3-2 Leicester City
1966:	West Bromwich Albion 5-3 West Ham United
1967:	Queens Park Rangers 3-2 West Bromwich Albion
1968:	Leeds United 1-0 Arsenal
1969:	Swindon Town 3-1 Arsenal

England 1966
Alf Ramsey

Key Players: Bobby Charlton (inside-forward), Geoff Hurst (striker), Bobby Moore (centre-half)

Trophies: World Cup 1966

Alf Ramsey's last game as an England player was the humiliating defeat at Hungary's hands at Wembley in 1953. It was a night that changed much in English football's mentality, but Ramsey did not succeed as England manager by simply copying the tactics the 'Magical Magyars' had brought to London. He realised that Hungary's greatest strength had been the way they tailored a system to suit the skills of the personnel they had, rather than the other way round.

The Wingless Wonders

Thirteen years later, England's managerial mastermind would plot World Cup victory by pioneering a system which today is the most popular in the English game: 4-4-2. Ramsey's team were known as 'wingless wonders' because they dispensed with the typically British inside-rights and inside-lefts and instead forged a cohesive midfield unit in which the emphasis was on technical excellence rather than speed. Martin Peters and Alan Ball were the men chosen to play on the wings, but they spent much of their time cutting inside and coming through the middle, which Ramsey felt was the best route to goal. The tactics confused opposing full-backs, who did not know whether to man-mark the 'wingers' or leave them to the centre-backs, which often led to England being able to outnumber opponents in the centre.

Working Hard

Ball and Peters were chosen for their roles because they worked hard and were not afraid to track back and help in defence, if needed. In the centre of midfield, Nobby Stiles would often play in front of the back four, covering plenty of ground and making vital last-ditch tackles, allowing Bobby Charlton to support the attacks. With the world's

Bobby Moore is immortalised with his World Cup team.

On Top Of The World in every sense after the World Cup victory.

finest goalkeeper, Gordon Banks, providing a pair of safe hands at the back and Bobby Moore marshalling the defence, England did not concede a goal until the semi-finals. In the quarter-finals, they showed their resolve by defeating Argentina in one of the toughest-ever World Cup clashes (Ramsey refused to let his players swap shirts with opponents he considered 'animals'), but against Portugal in the semis they showed their more skilful side to shatter Eusebio's dream.

It Came Home

The final piece of Ramsey's jigsaw came together in the final, when Hurst – the in-form but under-rated striker he had backed to take over from the injured Jimmy Greaves – played the game of a lifetime to send West Germany home. Even the normally taciturn Ramsey allowed himself to celebrate at the final whistle.

Manchester United 1968
Matt Busby

Key Players: George Best (winger), Bobby Charlton (inside-forward), Alex Stepney (goalkeeper)

Trophies: European Cup 1968

Matt Busby spent the decade which followed the Munich disaster rebuilding his Manchester United team, culminating in the European Cup win of 1968, which was arguably the club's finest hour and one which secured their place in legend.

Dazzling Duo

It set United on the road to becoming the most popular club in the world through its mix of tragedy, drama and emotion: from Busby picking himself up off his sick bed determined not to let the bloodshed of Munich be the end of United; through to the dawn of a new era for the club courtesy of the flamboyant brilliance of George Best. And yet perhaps the most important figure in United's European Cup victory, the first ever for an English club, was one of the players who survived Munich: Bobby Charlton. Busby knew Charlton was a player he could rely on to carry out his instructions to the letter, and an individual with enough skill and attacking flair to unlock even the most stubborn of defences. The manager was happy for the focus to fall on Best: while teams were busy watching the Ulsterman's dazzling footwork, sending two or even three players to mark him, it left more space for Charlton to exploit. And with skills like Best's, no number of defenders would stop him anyway.

Conquering Europe

Busby's plan to conquer Europe was a simple one – to unleash the attacking talents of Best, Charlton and (for most of the tournament) Denis Law, playing an up-tempo game as far up the field as possible, pressurising defences into mistakes and using Nobby Stiles and Pat Crerand to head off any counter-attacks. These two tough tacklers were the ideal foils for the fleet-footed forwards in front of them, and took the pressure off the defence. And in Alex

Stepney, United had one of the world's most reliable goalkeepers, a physically imposing custodian with few obvious weaknesses. In the European Cup final, Busby's plan worked perfectly: Charlton got behind the Best-

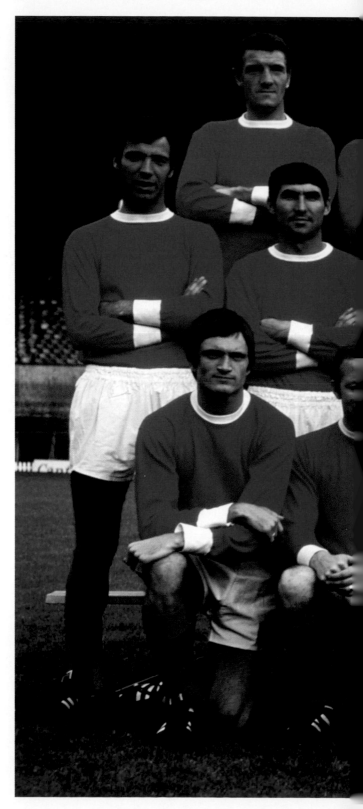

fixated defence to score in normal time, and when the Benfica players began to tire in extra time, Best stepped up a gear, scoring a sublime goal to give the English side the lead. A new 'Busby Babe', Brian Kidd, sealed the

victory, while another Munich survivor, Bill Foulkes, was imperious in defence having been handed an emotional recall to the side. It was Best's finest hour, but Busby's too – and for United, it was only the beginning....

The 1968 Manchester United players with Matt Busby. This team won the European Cup for their colleagues who died at Munich.

Leeds United 1968–75
Don Revie

Key Players: Billy Bremner (midfielder), John Giles (winger), Jack Charlton (centre-half)

Trophies: Football League 1969, 1974; FA Cup 1972; League Cup 1968; Fairs Cup 1968, 1971

Don Revie's transformation of Leeds United did not occur overnight, but it was eventually to reap spectacular rewards. When Revie was appointed in 1961, his playing days at Elland Road having come to an end, he was put in charge of a club lacking in finance and direction.

A New Direction

Leeds had almost dropped into the Third Division the previous season, but Revie turned the whole mentality of Elland Road around, starting with the playing kit – he introduced white shirts to ape those of Spanish giants Real Madrid, and drilled into his players the self-belief they needed to take the First Division by storm. Having reached the top flight in 1964, Revie set about creating a team which was physical (many would claim over-physical at times) and single-minded about winning. The trophies began in 1968 when a Terry Cooper goal landed Leeds the League Cup with victory over Arsenal, and weeks later Ferencvaros of Hungary were defeated to bring the Fairs Cup (forerunner of the UEFA Cup) to Yorkshire.

Teamwork

Revie had blended products of the club's excellent youth policy with a number of astute buys. He relied on grit in the centre of midfield, where Billy Bremner and Norman Hunter were a formidable pairing, Johnny Giles and (later) Peter Lorimer providing the flair. Jack Charlton was an inspiration in the centre of defence, and Terry Cooper and Eddie Gray combined brilliantly on the left. In 1970, Leeds boasted 17 internationals on their books. In 1969, they had romped to the First Division title, conceding just 26 goals as they amassed 67 points (a record in the days of two points for a win), and remaining unbeaten at Elland Road. In the summer, Revie broke the British transfer fee record by spending £165,000 on Leicester striker Allan Clarke, and the ace goalpoacher gave Leeds an even greater cutting edge. Another Fairs Cup followed, as did an FA Cup in 1972, when Clarke's goal saw off Arsenal. Leeds developed a bitter rivalry with the southern 'fancy dans' of Chelsea, whose stylish reputation was trampled in a number of brutal battles with grittier northerners.

At The Top Of Their Game

Revie's team reached their peak in 1974, remaining undefeated until February as they won the title again, but that summer their manager quit to take the England job and the board overlooked Giles as his replacement, appointing Brian Clough for a mere 44 days. Jimmy Armfield took Leeds to the European Cup final, where they lost in controversial circumstances, in 1975, but it would be some time before the club was challenging for the biggest honours again.

Leeds United celebrate with the League Cup after their win against Arsenal, 2 March 1968.

FEATURES

The World Cup Legend

Was England's 1966 World Cup victory the start of a golden age for English football or a poisoned chalice for the national game in decades to come?

Off The Pitch

In the short term, at least, victory had an invigorating effect on football: participation among youngsters rocketed, and attendances over the next couple of seasons picked up across all Football League divisions having been in freefall during the mid-1960s. Football established itself on television and begun

A poster advertising the World Cup.

to become more commercially aware as interest grew: much of the country had not seen matches live on TV before the tournament and found themselves enchanted by the drama they saw unfolding live and (often) in colour.

On The Pitch

Yet on the pitch, the World Cup win has become a millstone for successive England teams: at the 1986 World Cup, captain Bryan Robson said he 'hated' the image of Bobby Moore raising the Jules Rimet Trophy aloft, as it was used as a constant reminder of the legacy his new England side was struggling to live up to. At each major tournament since

Fans at Goodison Park cheer on League Division One Everton.

Bobby Moore shows the trophy to the world in the greatest moment in English footballing history.

1966, the World Cup win has been used as a backdrop to any discussion of England's chances, and players have admitted they have felt under pressure as media and supporter expectations were heaped on them.

A Millstone

For the heroes of 1966, too, the post-World Cup era was a mixed bag: Geoff Hurst noted feeling he had achieved everything he could in the game despite his relative youth, and the malaise even extended as

far as Sir Alf Ramsey himself: though he continued in the England hot seat for eight more years, many felt the Football Association was reluctant to be seen to dismiss the architect of England's finest hour. The memories of 1966 are unlikely to fade any time soon – which means a new era of England players will need to land a major title before the ghosts of that day at Wembley can truly be banished.

The England team, November 1966.

Modernisation Of Football

The point where football entered the commercial age is often pinpointed as England's World Cup win, but in fact it was three months earlier that the game first became big business. That was when Manchester United beat Benfica 5-1 in Lisbon, courtesy of George Best's dazzling dribbling, which ran the Portuguese team ragged.

Their Best Man

Best was already big news, but after that performance he made it onto the front pages, wearing a sombrero, and was christened 'El Beatle'. Bestmania was beginning to rival Beatlemania, with sackloads of mail arriving at Old Trafford and hordes of fans following the new superstar everywhere he went. Best was good-looking and did not always do what

George Best.

he was told: coupled with his natural talent, it made him perfect for the marketing men. He signed deals to promote books, posters, records and a host of other items, but he was not the only one who began cashing in: as more top players gained agents, particularly in the mid-1960s, they were able to secure deals outside the game which eclipsed their earnings from playing football.

Nice Little Earner

Johnny Haynes recounted how, when he took over from Denis Compton as the 'Brylcreem Boy', he earned 50 per

Tom Finney, Johnny Haynes, Stan Mortensen, Geoff Hurst, Bobby Moore and Alan Mullery line up for *A Question of Sport*.

Everton's Roger Kenyon challenges Dave Thomas of Queens Park Rangers.

cent more from three days' modelling than he did from a month's wages from Fulham, even after the abolition of the maximum wage. Other players wrote newspaper columns, appeared on TV quiz shows and comedies or launched their own clothing labels, and Peter Osgood reached a new level of fame when he was photographed with Raquel Welch and met Steve McQueen as a host of celebrities began flocking to Stamford Bridge to see the famous cosmopolitan Chelsea side of the 1960s.

Going Commercial

While working-class supporters were not yet being priced out of the game, there was a definite shift, particularly in the capital, towards more affluent crowds, and clubs began to undertake their own commercial activities by selling advertising hoardings around the pitch and, later, taking on club sponsors whose names were emblazoned on shirts. Spin-off merchandise, from replica kits to cuddly toys, began to appear in the 1970s: clubs were beginning to operate more like businesses, and players sought to maximise their earnings, moving from being mere professionals into a

moneyed elite more akin to showbusiness. It was a time of rapid change which would eventually elevate football to a multi-billion pound industry.

Fashion icon of the 1970s – George Best.

1970-83

Today, fans look back fondly on the 1970s as an innocent era of comical haircuts and ludicrous kits, but not everything in the garden was rosy. Hooliganism was on the rise, and it is no coincidence that attendances were also falling significantly as many of the new supporters attracted to the game in the wake of 1966 began to turn their backs on it as the atmosphere at matches became more hostile.

On the pitch, Chelsea and Leeds began the decade with a titanic Cup final battle and would clash many times in the coming years. England went home from the World Cup empty-handed after their own battles with Brazil and West Germany. Increasing commercialism helped fuel transfer inflation, and by 1979 Trevor Francis had become the first £1 million player.

Managers became more prominent personalities as the media increasingly sought their views, and two in particular – Bob Paisley and Brian Clough – would define the era. Clough took an unfashionable Nottingham Forest team to back-to-back European Cups, while Paisley stepped out of Bill Shankly's shadow at Liverpool to build a team which would enjoy unprecedented domestic dominance during the 1980s.

EVENTS

1971:
Arsenal Win The Double

Ten years after they became the first team of the twentieth century to do the double, Tottenham played an unfortunate role as their great north London rivals Arsenal repeated the feat. The Gunners went to White Hart Lane on the last day of the league season one point behind Leeds United, but knowing victory or a goalless draw (but not a scoring draw, thanks to the goal average rulings) would guarantee them the title.

In dramatic circumstances, Arsenal left it until the 87th minute to win the title on their bitter enemies' ground, Ray Kennedy's header ensuring the trophy was heading to Highbury. Bertie Mee's team deserved their achievement, as they boasted quality from back to front: from the faultless

Bob Wilson in goal, through defensive rock Frank McLintock and playmaker George Graham to the enigmatic talents of the great Charlie George. Liverpool stood in the way of the double at the FA Cup final, but in a tense and tight encounter it was George who grabbed the winner in a 2-1 victory. A quarter of a million people took to the streets of Islington to see the team take the trophies home, in what ranks among the club's finest hours.

1979:
The First £1 Million Player

At the start of the decade, the British transfer record stood at the £165,000 Leeds United paid for Allan Clarke in 1969, but over the next nine years it took a

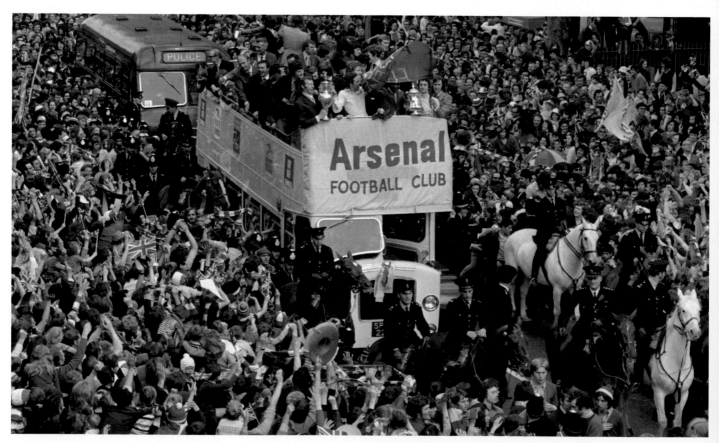

Ecstatic Arsenal fans are held back by mounted police as they crowd round the triumphal bus after the team wins the double.

Trevor Francis, the man who became the first £1 million player.

series of massive leaps as sponsor money and increased investment sent transfer inflation spiralling.

Derby's David Nish was the first £250,000 player in 1972, and Kenny Dalglish went for £440,000 in 1977. In December 1978, David Mills joined West Brom in the first half-million pound transfer, but just two months later that record was to be doubled as Brian Clough paid £1 million for 25-year-old striker Trevor Francis, Birmingham's scoring sensation and England international. Clough was chasing the title, and Birmingham were strapped for cash, but the move caused uproar and prompted many newspaper pundits to predict the game would implode should such transfers continue. Francis paid back a slice of the debt a few months later, when his goal gave Forest the European Cup with a win over Malmo of Sweden.

In September that year, Steve Daley joined Manchester City from Wolves for £1.43 million and it seemed the game truly had gone mad – especially as Daley, though a useful player, was not even an England international. He left City a year later for just £300,000.

FA CUP WINNERS

1970:	Chelsea 2-2 Leeds United Replay: Chelsea 2-1 Leeds United
1971:	Arsenal 2-1 Liverpool
1972:	Leeds United 1-0 Arsenal
1973:	Sunderland 1-0 Leeds United
1974:	Liverpool 3-0 Newcastle United
1975:	West Ham United 2-0 Fulham
1976:	Southampton 1-0 Manchester United
1977:	Manchester United 2-1 Liverpool
1978:	Ipswich Town 1-0 Arsenal
1979:	Arsenal 3-2 Manchester United
1980:	West Ham United 1-0 Arsenal
1981:	Tottenham Hotspur 1-1 Manchester City Replay: Tottenham Hotspur 3-2 Manchester City
1982:	Tottenham Hotspur 1-1 Queens Park Rangers Replay: Tottenham Hotspur 1-0 Queens Park Rangers
1983:	Manchester United 2-2 Brighton and Hove Albion Replay: Manchester United 4-0 Brighton and Hove Albion

PLAYERS

Viv Anderson (b. 1956)

(P: Nottingham Forest, Arsenal, Manchester United, Sheffield Wednesday, Middlesbrough, England; P&M: Barnsley)

England's first-ever black player won his first cap when he faced Czechoslovakia at Wembley in 1978. Though Viv Anderson entered the record books that night, he became equally well known for being a dependable and tough-tackling right-back, and won the European Cup with Nottingham Forest a year later. Anderson spent the 1980s with Forest, Arsenal and later Manchester United, where he became Alex Ferguson's first signing. He won 30 England caps, but went to the World Cups of 1982 and

The first black England player, Viv Anderson.

1986 without ever getting onto the pitch. He later became assistant manager of Middlesbrough when Bryan Robson was in charge of the Teeside club.

Ossie Ardiles (b. 1952)

(P: Huracan (Argentina), Tottenham Hotspur, Paris Saint Germain, Blackburn, Argentina; P&M: Swindon Town; M: Newcastle United, West Brom, Tottenham, Dinamo Zagreb, Shimizu S-Pulse (Japan))

A star of the 1978 World Cup, Osvaldo Ardiles caused a sensation when he and international team-mate Ricky Villa joined Tottenham when the tournament ended. The two Argentineans set the First Division alight with their skills and inspired Spurs to win the 1981 and 1982 FA Cups. When the Falklands War began the pair were sent home for diplomatic reasons, but Ardiles returned and lifted the UEFA Cup with Spurs in 1984.

He later became manager of Swindon Town and took them into the First Division in 1990, and managed gung-ho attack-minded Spurs and Newcastle teams in the same decade without significant success. He has since managed on four different continents.

Liam Brady (b. 1956)

(P: Arsenal, Juventus, Sampdoria, Inter Milan, Ascoli, West Ham, Republic of Ireland; M: Celtic, Brighton)

A brilliant midfielder with a superb range of passing, almost impossible to rob of the ball, Irish international Liam Brady enjoyed seven years with Arsenal, making 280 appearances in the famous red-and-white strip. He became a cult figure at Highbury after coming through the ranks, but he surprised many in 1980 by leaving for Italian giants Juventus. Brady's game was ideally suited to Serie A and he won the title twice with Juve before moving on to Sampdoria and Inter Milan, becoming one of the most acclaimed foreign imports in the Italian game at the time. He is now director of Arsenal's academy, developing young players to follow in his footsteps.

Billy Bremner (1942–97)

(P: Leeds United, Hull City, Doncaster Rovers, Scotland; M: Leeds, Doncaster)

A fiery character with a tough tackle and a passion for the game, midfield anchor Billy Bremner is widely regarded as Leeds United's finest-ever player. He made more than 700 appearances for the Elland Road club, and captained them to league titles in 1969 and 1974. In the 1974 Charity Shield, Bremner fought with Kevin Keegan and both players were dismissed in what became a famous incident of the time. Bremner was unable to repeat his success when he managed Leeds in the mid-1980s, but the way the city ground to a halt for his funeral in 1997 shows how highly regarded he was.

Below: Billy Bremner. Right: Liam Brady.

FOOTBALL WRITERS' ASSOCIATION FOOTBALLER OF THE YEAR

1970:	Billy Bremner	Leeds United
1971:	Frank McLintock	Arsenal
1972:	Gordon Banks	Stoke City
1973:	Pat Jennings	Tottenham Hotspur
1974:	Ian Callaghan	Liverpool
1975:	Alan Mullery	Fulham
1976:	Kevin Keegan	Liverpool
1977:	Emlyn Hughes	Liverpool
1978:	Kenny Burns	Nottingham Forest
1979:	Kenny Dalglish	Liverpool
1980:	Terry McDermott	Liverpool
1981:	Frans Thijssen	Ipswich Town
1982:	Steve Perryman	Tottenham Hotspur
1983:	Kenny Dalglish	Liverpool

Brian Clough
(1935–2004)

(P: Middlesbrough, Sunderland, England; M: Hartlepool, Derby, Brighton, Leeds, Nottingham Forest)

Quotable, opinionated and impossible to ignore, Brian Clough transformed Nottingham Forest into two-time European Cup winners through his impeccable motivation and his ability to spot talented young players. After his own prolific career was cut cruelly short by injury, Clough learned his trade at Hartlepool before winning Derby the 1972 league title. He lasted only 44 days at Leeds, but in 18 years at Forest he made the club his own, winning the 1978 title as well as four League Cups and his incredible European haul. He did it on a shoestring budget, and he did it with style: he would have walked into the England job had it not been for his many clashes with the FA.

Manager of the Year Brian Clough.

'I wouldn't say I was the best manager in the business, but I was in the top one,' he said, with typical modesty, when reflecting on his remarkable career.

Trevor Francis
(b. 1954)

(P: Birmingham, Nottingham Forest, Manchester City, Sampdoria, Atalanta, Rangers, Sheffield Wednesday; P&M: QPR; M: Sheffield Wednesday, Birmingham, Crystal Palace)

It is easy to suggest that Trevor Francis never quite lived up to his billing as Britain's first £1 million player, but though he only stayed at Nottingham Forest for two years following his remarkable 1979 transfer, his impact was still considerable: he had won Forest the European Cup within months, and only injury prevented him scoring more regularly. After a spell with Manchester City, Francis moved on to Italy and was later player-manager of QPR. Though his managerial record since has been patchy, he is best remembered as a pacy striker with a lethal finish.

Ron Greenwood (1921–2006)

(P: Chelsea, Bradford Park Avenue, Brentford, Fulham; M: West Ham, England)

While Alf Ramsey may have been England's manager in the 1966 World Cup, Ron Greenwood can share some responsibility for his country's success that year. As manager of West Ham from 1961, he nurtured the talents of Bobby Moore, Martin Peters and hat-trick hero Geoff Hurst, and also took the FA Cup and European Cup Winners' Cup back to Upton Park. Noted for his modern approach to fitness and tactics, he took over as England manager in 1977 and guided the team to two successive major finals, remaining unbeaten at the 1982 World Cup but still coming home after the group stages.

Left: Ron Greenwood. Right: Trevor Francis with the European Cup.

Alan Hansen (b. 1955)

(Partick Thistle, Liverpool, Scotland)

One of the finest centre-backs Britain has produced, Alloa-born Alan Hansen was Liverpool's defensive rock of the 1980s. A superb reader of the game, his tackling was always impeccable and his haul of eight league championships while at Anfield is a record he shares only with Phil Neal and Ryan Giggs. In 1986, Hansen captained Liverpool to the league and FA Cup double, but despite his consistent club form he was rarely first choice for Scotland and was left out of the 1986 World Cup finals squad by Alex Ferguson. He is now a popular and opinionated pundit on *Match Of The Day*.

Liverpool and Scotland player Alan Hansen in action.

Glenn Hoddle (b. 1957)

(P: Tottenham, Monaco, England; P&M: Swindon, Chelsea; M: Southampton, Tottenham, Wolves, England)

Although his managerial career has been mired by controversy, few could argue with Glenn Hoddle's command of a football. Few English players of any generation have been able to pass with such accuracy, over such distances, and Hoddle is widely acknowledged as one of the most cultured players Britain has ever produced. He came through the Tottenham ranks, making his debut in 1975 and later winning two FA Cups and the UEFA Cup before he joined Monaco. He won 53 international caps, a figure many believed should have been higher, but after taking over the England job himself in 1996 he was sacked three years later for comments he made about disabled people.

Pat Jennings (b. 1945)

(Watford, Tottenham, Arsenal, Northern Ireland)

One of very few players to be adored by fans of both Tottenham and Arsenal, Pat Jennings is rightly regarded as one of the best goalkeepers ever to play in the English top flight. The Northern Irish international spent 13 years at White Hart Lane, winning the 1967 FA Cup and the 1972 UEFA Cup, before making a controversial move to Highbury and picking up the 1979 FA Cup among his eight years with the club. For his country, Jennings appeared in two World Cups as a veteran, performing heroics against hosts Spain in 1982 as the Irish won 1-0, the most famous result in their history.

Kevin Keegan (b. 1951)

(P: Scunthorpe, Liverpool, Hamburg, Southampton, Newcastle, England; M: Newcastle, Fulham, Manchester City, England)

As popular for his relentless enthusiasm for the game as for his attacking flair, Kevin Keegan was England's main attacking threat during the 1970s and early 1980s – and he never let his country down. After coming through the ranks at Scunthorpe, Keegan was snapped up by Liverpool boss Bill Shankly in 1971 and was an England international by 1972. The title followed a year later, and Keegan played 230 times in all for the Reds before becoming a folk hero in Germany with Hamburg, twice being named European Footballer of the Year. He was similarly adored by Newcastle fans when he ended his playing career there, and as a manager later took them to the verge of beating Manchester United to the 1996 league title (complete with infamous 'I'd love it if we beat them … love it!' rant). His tenure with England was less successful, and he is now out of the game once more.

Kevin Keegan leads out his Liverpool team, 1976.

Arsenal and Northern Ireland goalkeeper Pat Jennings.

THE PFA PLAYERS' PLAYER OF THE YEAR

1974:	Norman Hunter	Leeds United
1975:	Colin Todd	Derby County
1976:	Pat Jennings	Tottenham Hotspur
1977:	Andy Gray	Aston Villa
1978:	Peter Shilton	Nottingham Forest
1979:	Liam Brady	Arsenal
1980:	Terry McDermott	Liverpool
1981:	John Wark	Ipswich Town
1982:	Kevin Keegan	Southampton
1983:	Kenny Dalglish	Liverpool

Bob Paisley (1919–96)

(P: Liverpool; M: Liverpool)

Bob Paisley stepped out of the shadows in 1974 to become one of the best-known managers in the English game. Paisley had a fine career as a player with Liverpool, which included the 1947 league title, and on retirement he took on a number of roles behind the scenes at Anfield, including physiotherapist, coach and assistant manager. When Bill Shankly retired, many doubted whether Paisley had a strong enough character to step into the hot seat, but he overshadowed his mentor's

England manager Don Revie.

achievements by winning three European Cups and six league championships as Liverpool became the team of the 1970s and 1980s. Adored at Anfield, Paisley was held in the highest respect by his players and is the most decorated club manager in the English game.

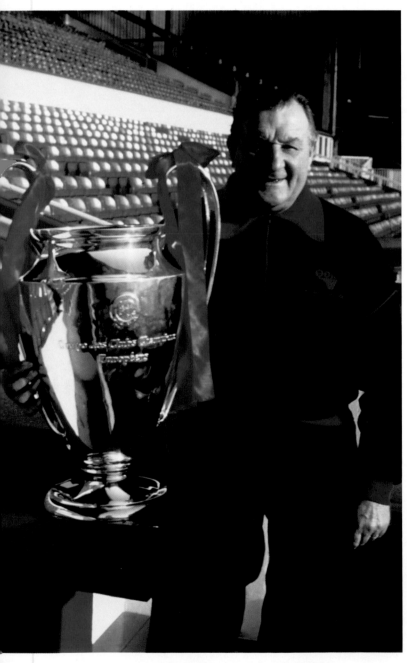

Liverpool manager Bob Paisley with the European Cup.

Don Revie (1927–89)

(P: Leicester, Hull, Manchester City, Sunderland, Leeds, England; M: Leeds, England)

The architect of Leeds' success in the 1970s, Don Revie built a team based on grit and hard work, and encouraged a siege mentality among his players which landed the club the first league titles of their history. Revie took over at Elland Road in 1961 and spent 13 years with the club, but he was a controversial figure to those outside Leeds, with his frequent outbursts and clashes with authority keeping him on the back pages. He was offered the England job in 1974, but made no significant inroads and left the country in disgrace three years later when he was offered a lucrative contract to coach in the United Arab Emirates.

One of England's finest goalkeepers, Peter Shilton.

Peter Shilton (b. 1949)

**(P: Leicester City, Stoke City, Nottingham Forest,
Southampton, Derby County, Bolton Wanderers,
Leyton Orient, England;
P&M: Plymouth Argyle)**

Peter Shilton was first choice throughout his career – and that record began when as a teenager he displaced Gordon Banks from the Leicester City team. Shilton was an agile, intelligent goalkeeper who inspired confidence in all those who played with him, and he made his England debut in 1970, gaining his first major silverware when he kept goal during Nottingham Forest's league and European Cup victories at the end of the decade. He won 125

England caps in total, being cruelly beaten by Diego Maradona's hand in 1986 and a deflection against West Germany in 1990.

In December 1996, he became the first player to appear in 1,000 professional matches in England, aged 47, when he appeared for Leyton Orient against Brighton.

Arnold Muhren (b. 1951)

(Ajax, FC Twente, Ipswich, Manchester United, Netherlands)

Frans Thijssen (b. 1952)

**(Vitesse Arnhem, FC Groningen, Fortuna Sittard,
Nottingham Forest, Ipswich Town, FC Twente, Netherlands)**

Foreign players were still rare in the late 1970s, but Ipswich boss Bobby Robson saw a major gamble pay off when two Dutchmen inspired his team to the UEFA Cup. Robson brought Arnold Muhren from FC Twente for £200,000 in 1978 and also signed his team-mate for the same amount. The two skilful midfielders gave Ipswich the cutting edge they needed and were outstanding as the Suffolk side beat Dutch team AZ Alkmaar to land the UEFA Cup. Thijssen was named Footballer of the Year that year, the first foreign player to win the award, and later won the 1988 European Championship, while Muhren went on to star for Manchester United.

Muhren and Thijssen – Bobby Robson's magical Dutch buy-in.

MATCHES

Carlos Alberto gets friendly with Bobby Moore, Brazil v. England.

in goal by David Harvey as a record 28 million tuned in on television. The move looked to have paid off when Mick Jones scored for Leeds after some brilliant play by Allan Clarke. The Yorkshire team were dominating the play, and were also winning the physical battle, which resulted in a number of punch-ups and brutal fouls: amazingly, there were no red cards. Chelsea carved out an equaliser with a Peter Osgood header into the second half, and then took the lead for the first time in either match when Dave Webb scored in extra time, holding on for an epic win.

Brazil 1-0 England
World Cup Finals, Guadalajara, Mexico, 7 June 1970

Brazil: (Man. Mario Zagallo) Felix, Carlos Alberto, Piazza, Brito, Everaldo, Clodoaldo, Paulo Cesar Lima, Jairzinho, Tostao (Roberto), Pele, Rivelino

England: (Man. Alf Ramsey) Banks, Wright, Cooper, Mullery, Labone, Moore, Lee (Astle), Ball, Charlton (Bell), Hurst, Peters

Scorer: Brazil: Jairzinho 60

Chelsea 2-1 Leeds United
FA Cup Final Replay, Old Trafford, 29 April 1970

Chelsea: (Man. Dave Sexton) Bonetti, Harris, McCreadie, Hollins, Dempsey, Webb, Baldwin, Houseman, Osgood (Hinton), Hutchinson, Cooke

Leeds: (Man. Don Revie) Harvey, Madeley, Cooper, Bremner, Charlton, Hunter, Lorimer, Clarke, Jones, Giles, Gray

Scorers: Chelsea: Osgood 78, Webb 104; Leeds: Jones 35

Though their performances were generally good, the World Cup of 1970 was not a happy one for England. The Mexican press did not make them welcome, captain Bobby Moore had been arrested on malicious charges of theft at Bogota airport in Colombia, and the oppressive heat in Guadalajara reduced the players to wrecks. Despite this, the holders put in a magnificent display in a classic match with Brazil, who would go on to win the tournament in style. Gordon Banks denied Pele in the tenth minute with what is regarded as one of the best saves of all time, and the great Brazilian enjoyed a battle of wits with Bobby Moore, who stood up to him throughout the game. Brazil got the winner on the hour after a brilliant passing movement, but England still got out of the group stages after winning their final game against Czechoslovakia.

The Chelsea-Leeds rivalry had been simmering for some time, but it was ignited in spectacular style at Old Trafford in 1970. For the first time since 1912, the FA Cup final finished all-square, the two sides drawing 2-2 at Wembley to force a replay in Manchester. Gary Sprake, blamed for Chelsea's first goal in the first match, was dropped by Don Revie and replaced

Ron Harris brandishes the FA Cup.

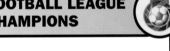

FOOTBALL LEAGUE CHAMPIONS

1970/71:	Arsenal
1971/72:	Derby County
1972/73:	Liverpool
1973/74:	Leeds United
1974/75:	Derby County
1975/76:	Liverpool
1976/77:	Liverpool
1977/78:	Nottingham Forest
1978/79:	Liverpool
1979/80:	Liverpool
1980/81:	Aston Villa
1981/82:	Liverpool
1982/83:	Liverpool
1983/84:	Liverpool

England 2-3 West Germany

World Cup Quarter Final, Leon, Mexico, 14 June 1970

England: (Man. Alf Ramsey) Bonetti, Newton, Cooper, Mullery, Labone, Moore, Lee, Ball, Hurst, Charlton (Bell), Peters (Hunter)

West Germany: (Man. Helmut Schön) Maier, Schnellinger, Vogts, Fichtel, Hottges (Schulz), Beckenbauer, Overath, Seeler, Libuda (Grabowski), Muller, Lohr

Scorers: England: Mullery 32, Peters 50; West Germany: Beckenbauer 69, Seeler 82, Muller 106

West Germany were itching for revenge when they met England in the quarter-final, and they were to get it over the course of 120 hard-fought minutes, to send the holders home in the cruellest way. England were 2-0 up by half time thanks to Alan Mullery and Martin Peters, but they began to tire as the match wore on, their energy sapped by the battle with Brazil. Germany were given a route back in on 69 minutes, when Peter Bonetti, playing in place of the unwell Gordon Banks, made a mess of a Franz Beckenbauer shot, and Uwe Seeler's header later levelled the tie. Gerd Muller, who would go on to win the 1970 Golden Boot, grabbed an extra-time winner.

Colchester United 3-2 Leeds United

FA Cup Fifth Round, Layer Road, 13 February 1971

Colchester: (Man. Dick Graham) Smith, Cram, Hall, Gilchrist, Garvey, Kurila, Lewis, Simmons, Mahon, Crawford, Gibbs

Leeds: (Man. Don Revie) Sprake, Reaney, Cooper, Bates, Charlton, Hunter, Lorimer, Clarke, Jones, Giles, Madeley

Scorers: Colchester: Crawford 18, 28, Simmons 49; Leeds: Hunter 60, Giles 78

In 1971, Leeds were at the height of their powers and were challenging for the First Division title, but they were brought down to earth with a bang at Fourth Division Colchester United in the Fifth Round of the FA Cup. Leeds, a team packed with internationals, were expected to wipe the floor with the Essex team, which included a number of veteran journeymen, but they had reckoned without Ray Crawford, a former Ipswich striker with two England caps who swept Colchester into a two-goal lead. Dave Simmons added a third, but Leeds rallied in the second half and pulled two goals back to produce what Crawford called 'the longest 12 minutes of my life' before a sensational giant-killing was confirmed.

Hereford United 2-1 Newcastle United

FA Cup Third Round, Edgar Street, 5 February 1972

Hereford: (Man. Colin Addison) Potter, Gough, Mallender, Jones, McLaughlin, Addison, George, Tyler, Meadows, Owen, Radford

Newcastle United: (Man. Joe Harvey) McFaul, n/k, n/k, n/k, Moncur, n/k, n/k, n/k, Macdonald, Tudor, n/k

Scorers: Hereford: Radford 86, George extra-time; Newcastle: MacDonald 82

One of the most famous giant-killings in FA Cup history, non-league Hereford's defeat of First Division Newcastle was made all the more famous by debutant pundit John Motson's commentary on *Match Of The Day*. The game was a replay, Hereford having already secured a creditable draw at St James' Park, but when

Malcolm Macdonald put Newcastle ahead on 82 minutes, it seemed Hereford's dream would be over. That was until Ronnie Radford slammed the ball home from 35 yards out, as Motson screamed 'What a goal! What a goal!' and hundreds of fans invaded the pitch. Shattered Newcastle were then undone in extra time by Ricky George's winner.

Colchester United try to hang on to their lead.

Left: Gerd Müller smashes the winning goal in Mexico, 1970.

Arsenal 3-2 Manchester United
FA Cup Final, Wembley, 12 May 1979

Arsenal: (Man. Terry Neill) Jennings, Rice, Nelson, Talbot, O'Leary, Young, Brady, Sunderland, Stapleton, Price (Walford), Rix

Manchester United: (Man. Dave Sexton) Bailey, Nicholl, Albiston, McIlroy, McQueen, Buchan, Coppell, Greenhoff, Jordan, Macari, Thomas

Scorers: Arsenal: Talbot 12, Stapleton 43, Sunderland 89; Manchester United: McQueen 86, McIlroy 88

Often described as the most dramatic FA Cup final of all time, Arsenal's last-gasp victory in 1979 would have seemed far-fetched in a Hollywood blockbuster. The Gunners' brilliant young midfielder, Liam Brady, had set up two goals in the first half, as Stewart Talbot and Frank Stapleton netted. United seemed dead and buried as Arsenal controlled the second half, but they took their foot off the gas too soon and with four minutes left, Gordon McQueen pulled one back before Sammy McIlroy equalised. Some teams might have been broken by such a

turnaround, but Arsenal went straight back up the other end and grabbed a last-minute winner, Brady again supplying the pass for Alan Sunderland to score.

Tottenham 3-2 Manchester City
FA Cup Final Replay, Wembley, 14 May 1981

Tottenham: (Man. Keith Burkinshaw) Aleksic, Hughton, Miller, Roberts, Perryman, Villa, Ardiles, Archibald, Galvin, Hoddle, Crooks

Manchester City: (Man. John Bond) Corrigan, Ranson, McDonald (Tueart), Caton, Reid, Gow, Power, MacKenzie, Reeves, Bennett, Hutchison

Scorers: Tottenham: Villa 8, 76, Crooks 76; Manchester City: Mackenzie 11, Reeves 50 (pen)

The FA Cup final of 1981 was the hundredth since the competition began, but this uniquely English occasion had a distinctly foreign flavour. Man City's Tommy Hutchison had the distinction of scoring at both ends as the first match ended 1-1, but in the replay

Arsenal celebrates. Back (l-r): Walford, Price, Jennings, Young, Sunderland, O'Leary. Front: Brady, Rice, Nelson, Talbot, Stapleton, Rix.

A victorious Spurs celebrates with the FA Cup trophy after defeating Manchester United 3-2 in 1981.

Tottenham's dazzling Argentinean Ricky Villa (aided by compatriot Ossie Ardiles) took control, giving Spurs the lead on eight minutes. Steve MacKenzie equalised, and Kevin Reeves put the northerners ahead from the spot after half-time, before Garth Crooks levelled the match again. Less than a minute later, Villa waltzed through the defence, rounded goalkeeper Joe Corrigan and scored one of the greatest cup final goals in history.

Norway 2-1 England
World Cup Qualifier, Oslo, 9 September 1981

Norway: (Man. Tor Røste Fossen) Antonsen, Berntsen, Aas, Hareide, Grondalen, Thoresen, Albertsen, Giske, Lund (Dokken), Okland (Pedersen), Jacobsen

England: (Man. Ronald Greenwood) Clemence, Neal, Mills, Osman, Thompson, Robson, Keegan, Francis, Mariner (Withe), Hoddle (Barnes), McDermott

Scorers: Norway: Albertsen 36, Thoresen 41; England: Robson 15

England made it through to the World Cup finals despite defeat in Norway, but their confidence took a major dent as they were beaten by a side they had thrashed 4-0 at Wembley the previous year. Bryan Robson put the visitors 1-0 up and they looked to be cruising, but Roger Albertsen and Hallvar Thoresen gave Norway a half-time lead they dug in deep to hold on to. Radio commentator Bjorge Lillelien entered folklore for his rant on the final whistle, reeling off a list of English historical figures before concluding '… your boys took a hell of a beating. Maggie Thatcher – Norway have defeated England! We are the world's best!'

Norway celebrates a surprise win over England.

TEAMS

Liverpool 1979–90
Bob Paisley, Joe Fagan, Kenny Dalglish

Key Players: Ian Rush (striker), John Barnes (winger), Kenny Dalglish (player-manager)

Trophies: Football League 1979, 1980, 1982, 1983, 1984, 1986, 1990; FA Cup: 1986, 1989; European Cup 1981, 1984; League Cup 1981, 1982, 1983, 1984

The Liverpool team of the 1980s was the most decorated club side the country had ever seen, and arguably its greatest ever. During this period, Anfield saw three different managers, but at no point did the trophies stop rolling in: this can be attributed to the famous 'Boot Room' approach at Liverpool, which saw managers promoted from within and backroom staff stay the same, so the philosophy at the heart of the club always remained unbroken.

FOOTBALL LEAGUE CUP WINNERS

1970:	Manchester City 2-1 West Bromwich Albion
1971:	Tottenham Hotspur 2-0 Aston Villa
1972:	Stoke City 2-1 Chelsea
1973:	Tottenham Hotspur 1-0 Norwich City
1974:	Wolverhampton Wanderers 2-1 Manchester City
1975:	Aston Villa 1-0 Norwich City
1976:	Manchester City 2-1 Newcastle United
1977:	Aston Villa 0-0 Everton Replay: Aston Villa 1-1 Everton Replay: Aston Villa 3-2 Everton
1978:	Nottingham Forest 0-0 Liverpool Replay: Nottingham Forest 1-0 Liverpool
1979:	Nottingham Forest 3-2 Southampton
1980:	Wolverhampton Wanderers 1-0 Nottingham Forest
1981:	Liverpool 1-1 West Ham United Replay: Liverpool 2-1 West Ham United
1982:	Liverpool 3-1 Tottenham Hotspur
1983:	Liverpool 2-1 Manchester United

In The Boot Room

This mentality was fostered in the club's boot room, where senior management and selected playing staff would meet in secret to make key decisions. Bob Paisley was a boot-room stalwart when he took over from Bill Shankly, and by 1979 the team he built was conquering everything in its path. That season, they conceded only 16 goals as they won the league with 68 points, and defended it successfully a year later. Alan Kennedy's goal handed the Reds the 1981 European Cup, and in 1982 they won back their league title despite being mid-table at Christmas. They also took the League Cup four times in a row – a remarkable achievement considering they had never before won the competition. Coach Joe Fagan stepped out of Paisley's shadow on his retirement, and despite never having managed before, the 63-year-old won the league at the first attempt and added the European Cup

A blanket of Liverpool red and white fills Wembley Stadium ahead of their FA Cup final against Arsenal.

for good measure, Kennedy scoring the shoot-out winner following Bruce Grobbelaar's goalkeeping heroics.

A Great Side

The Heysel disaster blunted Fagan's passion for the game, but any doubts about the abilities of Kenny Dalglish to follow him as player-manager were dispelled when he won the double in his first season, including a thrilling 3-1 cup final defeat of rivals Everton. Dalglish could still call on Alan Hansen to marshal his defence (his earlier partnership with Mark Lawrenson had been the best in English football) and Grobbelaar – despite his eccentricities and his habit of wandering from his goal-line and into trouble – was a brilliant shot-stopper. Although the likes of Steve Nicol and Ronnie Whelan may not have grabbed the headlines, their tough tackling and passing ability was at the heart of the Liverpool machine, as they played fluent pass-and-move

football which had the critics purring. Up front, Ian Rush's emergence as the greatest post-war domestic goalscorer was as good as giving Liverpool a goal start in matches, and Dalglish himself was still a thrilling sight in full flow; while Rush was in Italy, replacement John Aldridge was equally deadly. John Barnes, the most prominent black player in the English game, supplied a steady stream of crosses.

Another Tragedy

The ban on English clubs in the late 1980s stopped the Reds adding to their already impressive haul of European Cups. They won the title again in 1990, their 16th major trophy of the previous 11 years. Tragically, Hillsborough broke Dalglish just as Heysel had Fagan and Liverpool's dominance was at an end by the time he resigned in 1991 – but the memories of that era are still fresh in the minds of supporters.

Nottingham Forest 1978–90

Brian Clough

Key Players: Peter Shilton (goalkeeper), Martin O'Neill (midfielder), John Robertson (winger)

Trophies: Football League 1978; European Cup 1979, 1980; League Cup 1978, 1979, 1989, 1990

It is impossible to discuss the history of Nottingham Forest without one name looming large: Brian Clough. From the day he waltzed into the City Ground in 1975, he began remoulding the club in his own image: brash, flash and full of confidence, but also devastatingly effective.

Mr Motivator

Forest were a mid-table Second Division side when Clough joined them, but in 1977 he got them promoted and they took the First Division by storm. None of the Forest players were stars (save for England goalkeeper Peter Shilton, one of Clough's shrewdest buys), but with their manager's unusual motivational techniques and the air of invincibility he inspired in his players, they played out of their skins over the next three seasons.

The Clough Effect

Clough picked players who had been rejected elsewhere and turned them into winners, including veteran defender Larry Lloyd, Scottish midfielder Kenny Burns, free-scoring winger John Robertson, strikers Garry Birtles and Tony Woodcock and versatile midfielder Martin O'Neill. He also took two vital personnel with him from his previous championship win at Derby: captain John McGovern, an often-overlooked defender with strong leadership qualities, and long-time assistant Peter Taylor, a tactical genius and straight man to the eccentric manager. This unlikely crew was not expected to factor in the 1978 title race, having only finished third in the Second Division the previous year, but Forest were on fire and were crowned champions with four matches to spare.

Right At The Top

It was the start of a 42-game unbeaten run which took in the first 16 matches of the 1978/79 season, though they were to lose out to Liverpool that season. Consolation came in the form of the European Cup; record signing

Trevor Francis scored the only goal as Malmo were defeated 1-0 in Munich to leave the football world scratching its head in disbelief. Clough went one better and defended Europe's biggest trophy the following year, as John Robertson fired the winner against Hamburg. Had Liverpool not dominated the English game so thoroughly during the 1980s, Forest would have added to their haul

of major trophies, but they remained consistent top 10 finishers as new stars such as Stuart Pearce, Clough's son Nigel and, later, Roy Keane emerged.

Unique Achievement

Clough never landed the FA Cup, missing out in the 1991 final, and as his health deteriorated (culminating in his

punching two supporters who invaded the pitch, although he later kissed and made up with them live on national television) Forest were eventually relegated in 1993. Eight different managers have since tried and failed to emulate Clough's achievements with the club: it is unlikely any will ever succeed.

Nottingham Forest wins the European Cup.

Doncaster Belles
1983–94

Key Players: Gillian Coulthard (midfielder), Debbie Biggins (goalkeeper), Karen Walker (striker)

Trophies: National Premier League 1992, 1994; Women's FA Cup 1983, 1987, 1988, 1990, 1992, 1994

Women's football had been in existence since the earliest days of the game, but it took the emergence of a group of players from a Yorkshire pit town to bring it to national attention.

Forging Ahead

Following in the footsteps of the Dick Kerr Ladies – a Preston factory team who drew huge crowds to their exhibition matches during the First World War – the Doncaster Belles played an enormous role in popularising the female game and counteracting many of the negative comments and stereotypes which held back its development.

Competing At The Highest Level

The Belles were formed in 1969 by girls who sold raffle tickets at Doncaster Rovers matches; over the years, they grew into a fully fledged women's team and dominated regional competitions. They first won the Women's FA Cup in 1983 and have since appeared in the final a record 13 times, and when the National Premier League was formed in 1992 as the first official nationwide competition for women's teams, the Belles won the double at the first attempt. Star player Gillian Coulthard became the first woman to win a century of England caps, and to this day the club still competes at the highest level of the English game.

Charlton Athletic's Eniola Aluko and Doncaster Rovers Belles' Claire Utley battle for the ball in the Football Association's Nationwide Women's Premier League at Stonebridge Road.

Raising Their Profile

The Doncaster Belles became nationally recognised after author Pete Davies wrote *I Lost My Heart To The Belles* (1997), which told of the players' struggles for acceptance and showed the sacrifices they made and the difference the game made to their lives. It was followed by a television documentary which raised the club's profile even more.

Hooliganism

Crowd disturbances at football matches, contrary to the common perception, were not a phenomenon which developed in the 1960s and 1970s. In fact, the Riot Act had to be read to brawling spectators at public-school games in the 1840s, and in 1885 Preston players were forced to flee a 2,000-strong mob of Aston Villa fans who threw stones and missiles at them following a match.

Jubilant Scots destroy the goalposts after Scotland beats England, 1977.

Brewing Up Trouble

In the 1930s, several clubs, including QPR, had their grounds closed for a period of time as a punishment for crowd disorder, but the incidences of trouble became more regular in the 1960s, particularly among London clubs including Chelsea and Millwall. By the 1970s, a number of supporters, among them followers of Chelsea, West Ham and Stoke City as well as numerous others, had formed 'crews' or 'firms' who rampaged through town centres before matches and tried to infiltrate opposing

A Cheslea fan is led away by police after fighting in the terraces ruined the club's match against West Ham United in 1981.

supporters' areas at grounds. The 'football specials' trains which had been a popular and enjoyable way of travelling to games in the 1960s, soon became no-go zones as carriages were wrecked. At some First Division matches, seats were being ripped up and thrown at supporters, and the term 'hooligans' was being liberally applied to football fans by the popular press. There were also links between some hooligan elements and far-right parties, as witnessed in the abuse black players often received during the 1970s and 1980s. While much of the media-generated fervour about hooliganism blew the problem out of all proportion, it was a major blight on the game during this period and a major reason behind rapidly falling attendances.

Millwall Malaise

In the 1980s, the 'firms' become known as 'casuals' as they wore more nondescript clothing to evade the attention of police surveillance units, often staging organised fights away from town centres. The problem reached its peak in 1985, when the scenes of carnage at Heysel were preceded by a riot when Millwall visited Luton for an FA Cup quarter-final, hundreds of fans invading the pitch and staging a battle which saw dozens injured and 31 arrested, most of them supporters from London who had travelled as Millwall fans in the expectation of violence. One policeman almost lost his life, and 30 more were among

the injured as they tried to quell the riot. 'As a true Millwall fan it was impossible not to feel shame, not to feel sorrow for the game of football,' reported journalist James Murray. Luton banned away fans in the 1986/87 season, but a wider-ranging ID card system for fans, proposed by the Conservative government, was abandoned.

An End To Violence

Sadly, it took the Hillsborough Disaster and the advent of all-seater stadia to bring about the gradual cultural change which saw organised hooliganism dwindle, and by the turn of the new century it was restricted to sporadic outbreaks, mainly in the lower leagues and the non-league game.

Chelsea fans out of control again – in 1983.

Haircuts

Ever since footballers first became celebrities in their own right, putting their names to products and adorning schoolboys' sticker albums, they have sought to stay one step ahead of fashion in the hair stakes.

The Brylcreem Boys

Players' hair has gone through numerous cycles, almost all of them bad, reaching a nadir in the 1970s and 1980s which provokes hilarity among supporters who remember the halcyon days of perms and mullets. Today, David Beckham is a one-man hair industry, changing style dozens of times during his career in an effort to boost his profile. By endorsing Brylcreem in the 1990s, Beckham followed in the footsteps of Denis Compton, the former Arsenal player who began a trend for centre partings.

From The Sublime...

Players' hair before the 1960s was generally a conservative affair, though Billy Wright's ice cream cone-style quiff was considered adventurous. George Best aped the style of the Beatles in the 1960s and was christened 'El Beatle' himself, but team-mate Bobby Charlton was not as fortunate: as his hair disappeared in the 1970s, he took to combing what was left over the top of his head, thereby pioneering the comb-over style which would later be widely ridiculed.

Kevin Keegan never lived down his 1970s perm.

...To The Ridiculous

Charlie George, Arsenal hero of the 1970s, was the first big-name player to boast long hair, but come the 1980s two men would dominate the hair scene: Kevin Keegan and Chris Waddle. Keegan's perm grew more extravagant as the years went on, even partly obscuring his face at one point as he tried to storm the charts with 'Head Over Heels in Love' (1979). Waddle, a pop star in his own right after 'Diamond Lights' (1987) favoured the mullet, and his hair could often be seen flapping in the breeze behind him as he charged down the wing for Newcastle and Tottenham. At one point, Waddle even attempted to combine the mullet and the perm, with disastrous results: when he went to Marseille, French supporters began adopting his look in homage to his talents.

Style-Conscious

More recently, players have been too style-conscious to take significant risks with their hair, but David Seaman remained a notable exception during his tenure between the posts for Arsenal and England, gradually turning his unkempt mop into a pony tail which delighted opposing supporters.

Style-setters David Beckham (left) and George Best (above).

1984-91

It is difficult for even the most nostalgic football fan to look back on the 1980s as anything other than a dark time for the English game. The problem of hooliganism, which had been ignored by the authorities and leading clubs throughout the 1970s, grew progressively worse and the protagonists more organised in the early part of the decade, and tragedy soon followed as the Heysel Disaster led to a ban from European competition and placed a huge stain on the game.

The tragic occurrences at Hillsborough in 1989, though unrelated to hooliganism, further blackened football's mood, but forced the authorities to consider improving safety for spectators. The subsequent Taylor Report set in motion a chain of changes which would make the game safer and more pleasant for fans, provoking a surge of interest which would make it possible to form the Premier League in the early 1990s.

The European ban can also be said to have hindered the national team's development, although their two World Cup campaigns in this period ended in unfortunate circumstances – Maradona's Hand of God in 1986 being followed by penalty shoot-out hell in Italy four years later.

EVENTS

1984:
End Of Home Internationals

The so-called 'Home Internationals' or British Championships began life in 1883/84, when the respective Football Associations of England, Scotland, Wales and Ireland (later Northern Ireland) decided they should play an annual tournament. Each team would play every other team once in a league system; Scotland were the first victors, with a 1-0 victory over England in

Glasgow proving decisive. Over the next century, the title was competed for 89 times, although after the 1960s it was played in the course of a week at the end of the domestic season. By 1984, fixture congestion, for both clubs and national teams, spelled an end for the tournament, with Northern Ireland the victors on goal difference in the final championship after all four teams finished level on points.

The English FA felt England should concentrate on playing foreign teams to help improve their build-up for major tournaments, and hooliganism was also a factor – several matches had been blighted by crowd trouble,

including a pitch invasion by Scottish fans at Wembley in 1977 which had caused extensive damage. In all, England won more Home International titles than anyone else: 34, to Scotland's 24.

1985:
Heysel Stadium Disaster

Rising crowd violence in Britain and abroad had led many to fear a major disaster would take place at a football match, and those grim predictions were proved tragically correct at the 1985 European Cup final between Liverpool and Juventus. Poor crowd segregation and tickets being sold on the black markets meant both clubs' supporters were penned in together, and fighting broke out before kick-off. Missiles were thrown and a chicken-wire fence separating the two sets of supporters was ripped down as fighting broke out; a concrete wall collapsed on fleeing Italian fans. Thirty nine people died. The game went ahead almost 90 minutes late because police thought abandoning it would cause further violence; Juventus won 1-0 even though pitched battles were still occurring around the stadium and police had to patrol the perimeter to keep fans off the pitch. Fourteen Liverpool fans were later sentenced to three years for involuntary manslaughter.

Heysel is viewed as a particular low point in football history, and was one of the key factors in improving stadium safety and policing. In the wake of the disaster, English clubs were banned from European competition for five years by UEFA.

Chaos on the terraces at Heysel stadium. Thirty-nine people died.

FA CUP WINNERS	
1984:	Everton 2-0 Watford
1985:	Manchester United 1-0 Everton
1986:	Liverpool 3-1 Everton
1987:	Coventry 3-2 Tottenham Hotspur
1988:	Wimbledon 1-0 Liverpool
1989:	Liverpool 3-2 Everton
1990:	Manchester United 3-3 Crystal Palace Replay: Manchester United 1-0 Crystal Palace
1991:	Tottenham Hotspur 2-1 Nottingham Forest

1986:
Birth Of The Fanzine

The exact genesis of the football fanzine – a strictly amateur unofficial publication aimed at, and written by, supporters – is the subject of much debate, but it is clear that the phenomenon has become remarkably successful over the past 20 years, with every professional English club boasting at least one fanzine, and several claiming more than half a dozen. Fanzines are generally sold outside grounds on matchdays, or via subscriptions. Arsenal publication *Gunflash* often claims to be the first fanzine,

having been published since 1949, but it is produced by the official Arsenal Supporters Club so is not generally considered a fanzine. Bradford's *City Gent*, which first came out in 1984, has a stronger claim, while 1986 was the boom year for fanzines, with the biggest number of launches.

Inspired by punk fanzines of the late 1970s, the football fanzine craze was at its peak in the late 1980s and early 1990s, when new publications would appear on a weekly basis – only a limited number have survived unscathed. The magazine *When Saturday Comes* began life as a fanzine in 1986 (although it is now sold on national newsstands) and publicised many of the club-specific

Arsenal Ladies celebrate their Women's FA Cup win, May 2006.

fanzines available. The advent of the internet means many fanzines are now partly or wholly online.

1987:
Arsenal Ladies FC

The first women's team to be associated with a major men's club, Arsenal Ladies came into being in 1987 thanks to the efforts of Arsenal men's kit manager Vic Akers, who is also now the women's club's general manager. The team are affiliated with the men's club, although they are a separate entity, and are the most successful English club side with seven Premier League titles and six FA Cups since their inception. They supply several members of the England national team, including captain Faye White, the club's player-coach. Marianne Spacey, regarded as the best female footballer to come out of Britain to date, is a former Arsenal player and manager, and the team has twice reached the semi-finals of the Women's UEFA Cup, despite competing against professional teams, particularly those from Scandinavia who have many years' more experience in developing the women's game. Arsenal are regarded as the most advanced women's club in Britain, boasting the best facilities and coaching.

1989:
Hillsborough Disaster

English football's blackest hour occurred at the 1989 FA Cup semi-final between Liverpool and Nottingham Forest, and resulted in 96 deaths. The match, played at Sheffield Wednesday's Hillsborough stadium, was a keenly-awaited clash, and many of the Liverpool supporters were held up by traffic and reached the ground late. Huge queues developed around the turnstiles leading into the Leppings Lane terrace of the ground, and to ease them the police opened an exit gate to allow supporters in. Thousands rushed into the terrace, and it was soon dangerously full; as the game kicked off a crush began to develop, with supporters unable to escape because of the fences separating them from the pitch. Some climbed the fences and others were pulled into the upper tier of the ground by other fans, but many died in the crush. The referee stopped the game after six minutes, and the pitch began to fill with injured fans being carried away on advertising hoardings or awaiting medical treatment.

The subsequent Taylor Report put the official blame at the police decision to open the exit gates, but the disaster also provoked a long campaign from victims' families for an official enquiry into how the events occurred and the behaviour of the police on the day.

1990:
The Taylor Report

Lord Justice Taylor was asked by the Home Office to look into the Hillsborough Disaster and make recommendations to ensure such a tragedy was never repeated. His enquiry took a month, and its major finding was that in future all top-flight stadiums in England and Scotland should be all-seater: this would ensure that only the official capacity would ever be allowed into the ground, preventing any future crushing or large numbers of people arriving en masse in a particular section of a ground. The report also recommended fencing be removed from grounds at all levels, as this was a major contributory factor in the Hillsborough death toll. Over the next few years, clubs began removing their terraces and installing seats, at a huge financial cost.

Today, every Premiership and Championship club is all-seater by law, and terracing is gradually being phased out at many lower division clubs too. This is credited with having a huge effect on improving behaviour within

grounds and making football safer for supporters. However, many fans' groups claim all-seater grounds have ruined the atmosphere at matches, discouraging singing and giving clubs an excuse to hike ticket prices: some have

campaigned for the introduction of selected terraced areas, under strict conditions, but there is no sign the authorities are considering this move.

Tributes adorn the perimeter of the Hillsborough stadium.

PLAYERS

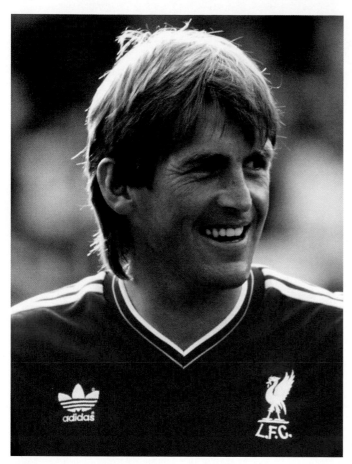

'King Kenny' was a Kop hero who is seen as Liverpool's greatest-ever player.

Kenny Dalglish (b. 1951)

(P: Celtic, Liverpool, Scotland; P&M: Liverpool; M: Blackburn, Newcastle, Celtic)

One of Scotland's finest-ever players and a hero both sides of the border, Kenny Dalglish was a boyhood Rangers fan but made his name with Celtic. The skilful striker was a great goalscorer but also an intelligent and unselfish player, and he was the ideal replacement when Kevin Keegan left Liverpool in 1977, filling the void to become an instant fans' favourite at Anfield. He won the 1977 European Cup for Liverpool and he stayed for 13 years, winning every honour in the English game first as a player, and later as player-manager. He left Liverpool soon after witnessing Hillsborough, but returned to management with Blackburn and won the Premiership in 1995.

George Graham (b. 1944)

(P: Aston Villa, Chelsea, Arsenal, Manchester United, Portsmouth, Crystal Palace, Scotland; M: Millwall, Arsenal, Leeds, Tottenham)

As a player, most notably with Arsenal from 1966–72, George Graham was known as 'Stroller' for his languid, occasionally lazy, playing style. A gifted inside-forward, he won only 12 caps for his country and was sold by Chelsea after breaking a curfew under Tommy Docherty. As a manager, his style could not have been more different: he was a strict disciplinarian who trained his players hard and did not tolerate rule-breaking, Graham took over at Arsenal in 1986 and is credited with turning the club around and leading them to two league titles by building a tight defensive unit. He left Highbury in 1995 after being involved in an illegal payments scandal, and controversially later managed rivals Tottenham.

Graham is credited with bringing some great players to Arsenal, including David Seaman.

Andy Gray (b. 1955)

(Dundee United, Aston Villa, Wolves, Everton, West Brom, Rangers, Scotland)

A brilliant and consistent goalscorer, Andy Gray went on to become the nation's best-known football pundit. He made his name with Aston Villa (he had two spells at Villa Park) and Wolves before moving to Everton in 1983, where he won his only major medals – the 1984 FA Cup and the 1985 First Division title and European Cup Winners' Cup. After ending his career, he helped launch Sky Sports' slick Premiership coverage in the early 1990s, using a variety of high-tech gadgets to demonstrate teams' tactical failings.

Vinnie Jones was infamous for his brutal 'hard man' image.

Vinnie Jones (b. 1965)

(Wimbledon, Leeds, Sheffield United, Chelsea, QPR, Wales)

Vinnie Jones' entry into top-flight football was probably the most unexpected ever. Playing in non-league football for Wealdstone and working on a building site, he was asked to train with former manager Dave Bassett, now in charge of First Division debutants Wimbledon, and within a week he was playing against Brian Clough's Nottingham Forest. A week later, he scored the winning goal against Manchester United. Jones' hard-man image and physical style made him notorious and he was sent off 12 times in his career (though he was not punished for famously grabbing Paul Gascoigne's private parts), but he also forged an international career with Wales and was the inspiration behind Wimbledon's 1988 FA Cup final win. After retiring from football, he became an actor, appearing in a string of Hollywood action movies.

After his outstanding 1977/78 season, Gray was made PFA Young Player of the Year.

FOOTBALL WRITERS' ASSOCIATION FOOTBALLER OF THE YEAR

1984:	Ian Rush	Liverpool
1985:	Neville Southall	Everton
1986:	Gary Lineker	Everton
1987:	Clive Allen	Tottenham Hotspur
1988:	John Barnes	Liverpool
1989:	Steve Nicol	Liverpool
1990:	John Barnes	Liverpool
1991:	Gordon Strachan	Leeds United

Matthew Le Tissier (b. 1968)

(Southampton, England)

One of the most enigmatic and popular players of his generation, Guernsey-born Matt Le Tissier is known to Southampton fans as 'Le God'. Almost uniquely among modern-day superstars, he spent his entire career on the south coast, emerging in 1986 and playing more than 500 times for Southampton. He almost joined Tottenham in 1991, but tore up his contract after his wife refused to move to London: by never leaving Southampton, he missed out on the chance to win any major honours. Le Tissier won 21 England caps, but critics claimed his poor work-rate cost him dearly, though in his day his ball skills were magical and his long-range passing and shooting was reminiscent of Glenn Hoddle.

Gary Lineker went 16 years without a single booking.

Gary Lineker (b. 1960)

(Leicester City, Everton, Barcelona, Tottenham, Grampus Eight (Japan), England)

Throughout his career as a player, pundit and television presenter, Gary Lineker has maintained an image as football's 'Mr Nice Guy'. Never booked during 16 years on the pitch, he was a deadly goalscorer both in the First Division and abroad. Although he was short on skill, Lineker had a knack for being in the right place at the right time and always hitting the target. He came through the ranks at hometown club Leicester before grabbing 30 league goals in a season for Everton. Lineker joined Terry Venables at Barcelona and was a sensation in Spain, also winning the Golden Boot at the 1986 World Cup. He scored 48 times in 80 appearances for his country and finished his career with Venables at Tottenham.

David O'Leary (b. 1958)

(P: Arsenal, Leeds, Republic of Ireland;
M: Leeds, Aston Villa)

David O'Leary's reputation as a defensive rock made him Arsenal's all-time record appearance holder, having played 722 times in all competitions for the club. He made his debut as a 17-year-old and was soon a first-team regular, keeping his place for 20 years, although he left

Matt Le Tissier, known to Southampton fans as 'Le God'.

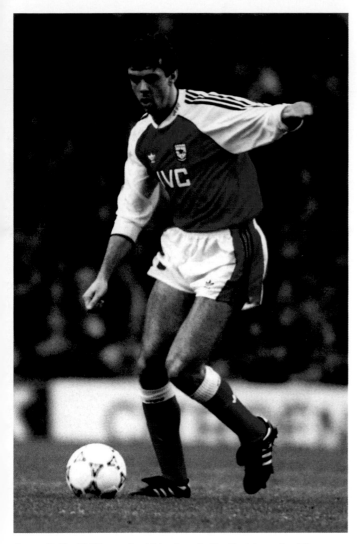

Arsenal's David O'Leary kept his place in the first team for 20 years.

Portugal, being named European Manager of the Year in 1997, but was unable to bring major trophies to his beloved Newcastle United.

Bryan Robson (b. 1957)

(P: West Brom, Manchester United, England;
P&M: Middlesbrough; M: Bradford City, West Brom)

Known as England's 'Captain Marvel' for his inspirational leadership and dedication to the cause, Bryan Robson's playing career was blighted by injury. He suffered almost every kind of injury a footballer can endure, but still made 90 appearances for his country, and once scored after just 27 seconds in the 1982 World Cup. He helped West Brom into the First Division before joining Manchester United in 1981 and became a legend at Old Trafford, finally winning the title with United in 1993. As a manager, he enjoyed a rollercoaster ride in charge of Middlesbrough and was later unable to keep West Brom in the Premiership.

it late to win major silverware, only winning the league title in 1989 and the FA Cup and league double in 1993. He scored the decisive penalty in Ireland's famous World Cup win over Romania in 1990, and as a manager came close to bringing major silverware to Leeds with a young team.

Sir Bobby Robson (b. 1933)

(P: Fulham, West Brom, England; M: Fulham, Ipswich,
PSV Eindhoven, Sporting Lisbon, Porto, Barcelona,
Newcastle, England)

Almost uniquely in football, Sir Bobby Robson is universally adored by players and supporters alike for his sense of humour, love of fair play and knowledge of the game. After a successful playing career which included 20 England caps, Robson won the FA Cup and UEFA Cup with Ipswich and almost took England to the 1990 World Cup final during eight years in charge of the national team. He enjoyed considerable success in both Spain and

Bobby Robson is respected for his love of fair play.

Liverpool's Ian Rush celebrates a goal in the 1986 FA Cup final against Everton.

Ian Rush (b. 1961)

(P: Chester City, Liverpool, Juventus, Leeds, Newcastle, Wrexham, Wales; M: Chester)

Ian Rush was quite simply the best and most prolific goalscorer in the British game. His 346 goals for Liverpool and 28 for Wales are both records, but he holds plenty more besides: five goals in FA Cup finals and 48 in the League Cup make him the highest scorer in both. He also won five league titles and three FA Cups with Liverpool during two legendary spells with the club in the 1980s, in between an unsuccessful season in Italy.

Midfielder Graeme Souness.

Graeme Souness (b. 1953)

(P: Tottenham, Middlesbrough, Liverpool, Sampdoria, Scotland; P&M: Rangers; M: Liverpool, Galatasaray (Turkey), Southampton, Torino, Benfica, Blackburn, Newcastle)

Graeme Souness might have become a vital part of Bill Nicholson's early 1970s Tottenham side, but left after a lack of first-team opportunities. Instead, the rugged, hard-tackling central midfielder became a legend at Liverpool, captaining the team to a number of major trophies in the 1980s, including two European Cups. After a spell in Italy, he entered management with Glasgow Rangers, winning the title four times after importing a number of English players, but was unable to replicate this success when he returned to Anfield.

Neville Southall (b. 1958)

(Bury, Everton, Southend, Stoke, Torquay, Bradford, Wales)

Despite his occasionally undignified style and huge frame, Neville Southall was arguably the finest goalkeeper in the world during the 1980s, performing acrobatics on a weekly basis as Everton claimed two league titles and an FA Cup. He made a club record 578 appearances for Everton, and is also Wales' most capped player, having played 93 times for his country. Famously gruff, he once sat against a goalpost with his arms folded for the entire half-time interval of an Everton match when he was unhappy with his side's first-half performance.

Graham Taylor

(b. 1944)

(P: Grimsby Town, Lincoln City; M: Lincoln, Watford, Aston Villa, Wolves, England)

Although he is often associated with a disastrous spell in charge of the England team, Graham Taylor's most notable managerial roles came with Watford and Aston Villa. At Vicarage Road, he took Watford from the Fourth Division to the First Division, finishing second in their first season in the top flight, 1982/83. He finished second with Aston Villa in 1990, before he took over from Bobby Robson with England but left after failing to qualify for the 1994 World Cup. He is associated with a direct style of play, and the infamous catchphrase 'Do I not like that'.

Graham Taylor made little impression as England manager.

Everton goalkeeper Neville Southall.

THE PFA PLAYERS' PLAYER OF THE YEAR

Year	Player	Club
1984:	Ian Rush	Liverpool
1985:	Peter Reid	Everton
1986:	Gary Lineker	Everton
1987:	Clive Allen	Tottenham Hotspur
1988:	John Barnes	Liverpool
1989:	Mark Hughes	Manchester United
1990:	David Platt	Aston Villa
1991:	Mark Hughes	Manchester United

MATCHES

Argentina 2-1 England
World Cup Quarter-Final, Mexico City, 22 June 1986

Argentina: (Man. Carlos Bilardo) Pumpido, Cuicuffo, Brown, Ruggeri, Olarticoechea, Batista, Giusti, Burruchaga (Tapia), Henrique, Valdano, Maradona

England: (Man. Bobby Robson) Shilton, Stevens, Sansom, Hoddle, Fenwick, Butcher, Hodge, Reid (Waddle), Beardsley, Lineker, Steven (Barnes)

Scorers: Argentina: Maradona 51, 54; England: Lineker 80

Rarely has a football match been mired in such controversy, or touched by such genius, as England's 1986 World Cup exit. The game was dominated by Diego

Maradona, who since emerging in the late 1970s had gradually become the most skilful player in the world. He would now become the most reviled man in England, as in the 51st minute of this quarter-final meeting he rose with goalkeeper Peter Shilton to meet a mis-hit Steve Hodge clearance which was heading into the penalty area. Maradona outjumped Shilton, but replays showed him very clearly punching the ball over the keeper and into the net; Maradona glanced at the Tunisian referee and, seeing no reaction, began celebrating.

He would later claim the 'Hand of God' had scored the goal, but the English players who chased furiously after the match official knew differently. Three minutes later,

Mexico 1986 – Diego Maradona became the focus of universal anger after his 'Hand of God' goal.

Arsenal's Niall Quinn, nicknamed 'Mighty', scores the team's second goal on his debut for them.

Maradona showed the other side of his nature by waltzing through the entire English defence to score one of the finest individual goals ever seen in a major tournament. Although Gary Lineker pulled a goal back, England had been left shattered by Maradona and Lineker spurned a late chance to equalise. It was a match which would be discussed for years, and which only intensified the rivalry between the two nations.

Liverpool 0-2 Arsenal
First Division, Anfield, 26 May 1989

Liverpool: (Man. Kenny Dalglish) Grobbelaar, Nicol, Hansen, Ablett, Staunton, Houghton, Whelan, McMahon, Barnes, Alridge, Rush (Beardsley)

Arsenal: (Man. George Graham) Lukic, Dixon, Winterburn, Adams, Bould (Groves), O'Leary, Merson (Hayes), Rocastle, Richardson, Thomas, Smith

Scorers: Arsenal: Smith 54, Thomas 90

Never has a title race been decided in such dramatic style as the 1989 one – and coming just a month after the Hillsborough Disaster, the scenes at

FOOTBALL LEAGUE WINNERS	
1984/85:	Everton
1985/86:	Liverpool
1986/87:	Everton
1987/88:	Liverpool
1988/89:	Arsenal
1989/90:	Liverpool
1990/91:	Arsenal
1991/92:	Leeds United

Anfield that night did much to help a grieving game begin refocusing on events on the pitch. Arsenal travelled north for the final fixture of the season in second position in the league, knowing only a victory by two clear goals would take the title away from a seemingly invincible Liverpool and send it to Highbury for the first time in 18 years.

Few gave them any chance of winning, but they gained some hope when Alan Smith put them ahead early in the second half. Arsenal poured forward, but Liverpool stood firm and the visitors were getting tired by the time Steve McMahon realised there was only a minute left and began telling his team-mates they only had to hold on for 60 seconds more. Kevin Richardson then won the ball in the Arsenal area and began a quick move upfield which ended with midfielder Michael Thomas being put clear and firing past goalkeeper Bruce Grobbelaar to send north London into rapture as million watched on television. The match would later be the backdrop for the successful book (1992) and film (1996), *Fever Pitch*.

Sutton United 2-1 Coventry City
FA Cup Third Round, Gander Green Lane, 7 January 1989

Sutton United: (Man. Barry Williams) Roffey, Jones, Rains, Golley, Pratt, Rogers, Stephens, Dawson, Dennis, McKinnon, Hanlan

Coventry City: (Man. John Sillett) Ogrizovic, Borrows, Phillips, Sedgely, Kilcline, Peake, Bennett, Speedie, Regis (Houchen), McGrath, Smith

Scorers: Sutton: Rains, Hanlan; Coventry: Phillips

Statistically, Sutton United's defeat of Coventry is the biggest shock in FA Cup history, given the chasm in league position between the teams. The Sky Blues had won the cup only two years previously and were sixth in the First

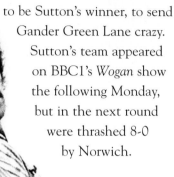

Division at the time. The part-time Surrey side were in the Conference but drew a record crowd of 8,000 for their big day. Tony Rains gave them the lead before David Phillips equalised for Coventry after the break. Computer programmer Matthew Hanlon bundled home what was to be Sutton's winner, to send Gander Green Lane crazy. Sutton's team appeared on BBC1's *Wogan* show the following Monday, but in the next round were thrashed 8-0 by Norwich.

England 1-1
West Germany
World Cup Semi-Final, Turin, 4 July 1990

England: (Man. Bobby Robson) Shilton, Pearce, Walker, Butcher (Steven), Parker, Wright, Waddle, Gascoigne, Beardsley, Lineker, Platt

West Germany: (Man. Franz Beckenbauer) Ilgner, Brehme, Kohler, Augenthaler, Berthold, Buchwald, Hassler (Reuter), Matthaus, Thon, Voller (Riedle), Klinsmann

Scorers: England: Lineker 80; West Germany: Brehme 59

England had their best chance since 1966 of lifting the World Cup in 1990, but were agonisingly defeated in what would be the first of several penalty shoot-out embarrassments. The dour but effective West German side gave the English a fascinating battle in a match best remembered for Paul Gascoigne's tears when he realised his yellow card meant he would miss the final, should England win. Andreas Brehme's deflected free-kick gave the Germans the lead, but Gary Lineker took the game into extra-time with a cool finish. With the shoot-out locked at 3-3, Stuart Pearce saw a weak spot-kick saved, and after Olaf Thon netted to make it 4-3, Chris Waddle blasted over the bar to send England home.

First Women's
World Cup, 1991

By 1990, the women's game was making huge strides in popularity across the world, and the 1991 World Cup was the first played as an official tournament under the direction of global governing body FIFA. England had won the unofficial 1985 and 1988 World Cups, but did not qualify for this enlarged competition, held in China, which attracted huge crowds, including 63,000 who turned up to see the final. The USA beat Norway 2-1 to lift the trophy thanks to two goals from Player of the Tournament, Michelle Akers.

Left: Paul Gascoigne despairs as West Germany give England a traditional routing in the 1990 World Cup semi-final.

Far left: Sutton United and Coventry City go head to head, January 1989.

TEAMS

Wimbledon 1988
Dave Bassett

Key Players: Dave Beasant (goalkeeper), Vinnie Jones (midfielder), John Fashanu (striker)

Trophies: FA Cup 1988

The Wimbledon story of the 1980s is one of the most romantic in English football, but its realisation also required a certain amount of brutality. It culminated in 1988 with the unlikeliest FA Cup final victory ever, as an assorted collection of players plucked from the lower divisions prevented the all-conquering Liverpool team from doing the double.

The Crazy Gang

The Dons had risen from the non-league game, first entering the league in 1978 and rising rapidly to reach the First Division by 1986. Their managerial mastermind was Dave Bassett, who created a 'Crazy Gang' spirit of outrageous pranks and bizarre rituals and was determined to take the football establishment by storm. He was aided by chairman Sam Hammam, who would often be found racing players across the training pitch for money, and promised a 'stream of blood from here to Timbuktu' should the club ever be relegated. Wimbledon played aggressive, route-one football of a kind few teams had encountered: they would play the ball high upfield at every opportunity, hoping to catch opponents on the break and outmuscle them to the ball. They had no respect for reputations, and amazed pundits by finishing sixth in their first season in the top flight.

A Motley Crew

In their rise through the divisions, they had picked up a number of remarkable characters, including Vinnie Jones, a tattooed former hod carrier who terrified opponents and John Fashanu, an imposing centre-forward with a reputation for injuring defenders who stood in his path. Eric Young and John Scales were capable centre-halves and Lawrie Sanchez was a workmanlike midfielder, while goalkeeper Dave Beasant was an expert at saving penalties. Even so, they were given little hope against Liverpool, even though the Dons (now managed by Bobby Gould) were again sitting in the top 10.

The Stuff Of Legend

Wimbledon had spent the previous night in the pub because their hotel was too boring, but they had no hangover; on 37 minutes, Sanchez nodded home Dennis Wise's free kick and the champions were stunned. On the hour, the Reds were awarded a penalty, but Dave Beasant made history as the first man to save an FA Cup final spot-kick at Wembley when he parried John Aldridge's effort. The Dons dug deep and held on for Beasant to become the first goalkeeper ever to lift the trophy. Commentator Barry Davies claimed 'The Crazy Gang have beaten the Culture Club' as the Dons celebrated the finest moment in their history.

The Wimbledon team celebrates its FA Cup final victory.

FOOTBALL LEAGUE CUP WINNERS

1984:	Liverpool 0-0 Everton
	Replay: Liverpool 1-0 Everton
1985:	Norwich City 1-0 Sunderland
1986:	Oxford United 3-0 Queens Park Rangers
1987:	Arsenal 2-1 Liverpool
1988:	Luton Town 3-2 Arsenal
1989:	Nottingham Forest 3-1 Luton Town
1990:	Nottingham Forest 1-0 Oldham Athletic
1991:	Sheffield Wednesday 1-0 Manchester United

FEATURES

Stadia Safety

A ban on English clubs competing in Europe was in force within weeks of the Heysel Disaster. It had the backing of the FA, UEFA and the government, and was seen as the only way to stop a similar incident occurring – as well as safeguarding the reputation of English football, which had been tarnished by a string of well-publicised hooliganism-fuelled scenes which had got increasingly worse throughout the 1980s.

Banishing Tragedy

The ban would last until 1990 (1991 for Liverpool) and would prevent three European Cup qualifications for the Reds and two for rivals Everton, as well as keeping Manchester United out of the UEFA Cup twice. But it was not just the biggest names in the game who missed out: Wimbledon, Luton, Oxford United and Coventry City would all have played in major European

Police face crowds of angry Liverpool fans as they try to control the fighting that has broken out in the stands at the Heysel stadium.

competitions for the first time in their histories had it not been for the ban. The tragedy at Hillsborough in 1989 forced football to consider stadium safety as a whole, rather than just focusing on crowd disorder. It was clear that all-seater stadia and improved safety features would be needed if such shocking events (and those at Bradford's Valley Parade in May 1985, when 56 people were killed in a fire started accidentally in an old wooden stand) were to be banished from the game forever.

All Sit

The Taylor Report's recommendations were implemented with immediate effect, and all Premiership clubs were all-seater before the 1995 deadline. Much of the funding for such a move came from the Football Foundation (funded by the government and pools companies), with the report making it clear that clubs should not raise admission prices significantly when seats became the norm: however, most clubs immediately raised their prices, and by 2005 the average seat at Chelsea was approaching £50, more than four times the level in 1990.

Rising Attendances

The Kop at Anfield and the Shed End at Chelsea were among the famous banks of terracing which disappeared in the change, but attendances rose as many people driven away from the game by negative publicity in the 1980s began to return to grounds. Improved stewarding implemented by clubs helped too, as did a friendlier atmosphere at matches which saw Manchester City fans bringing inflatable toys to games, sparking a nationwide craze. Much of the improved safety at matches from the 1990s onwards came from changes in fan culture as well as prize rises and an increase in older, more 'gentrified' supporters – the real tragedy is that it took such horrific scenes to force the game to change.

As the 1990s dawned people began to return to the terraces after the negative publicity of the disasters that had characterised the 1980s.

Women's Football

The women's game had existed in an organised way since the First World War (although the first recorded match was in 1895), when the Dick Kerr Ladies drew huge crowds in Preston at a time when the men's game had dwindled with so many players joining the forces. But while providing novelty wartime entertainment was one thing, in peacetime women's teams found it more difficult to be taken seriously.

Finding Their Feet

An intensely chauvinistic attitude prevailed in the game for the whole of the twentieth century, as characterised by Ron Atkinson's famous comment that 'a woman's place is in the boutique or the discotheque, not on the football pitch.' The FA even banned the women's game in 1921, finding it 'quite unsuitable'. Even so, thanks to the determined efforts of a number of pioneers, women's football did slowly develop, with 44 clubs forming the Women's Football Association in 1969, the same year as the first semi-official international match involving England. The first official fixture took place three years later, England beating Scotland 3-2 in Greenock, although the FA maintained a distance from the women's team for some time.

Above: England coach Hope Powell.

Below: The 1990 Women's Soccer FA Cup winners.

The 1999 Women's World Cup was a sell-out success.

Leagues Are Launched

It was the WFA that launched a national league in 1991, but soon growing interest – aided by the media coverage the Doncaster Belles were receiving – made it inevitable that the Football Association would take control, and the national league and cup competitions had become the Women's FA Cup and Football Association Women's Premier League respectively by 1994. Hope Powell became the first female England coach in 1998, and when England hosted the UEFA Women's European Championship in 2005 healthy crowds were drawn to North-West grounds, including 29,000 for England's opening game with Finland.

Send In The Professionals

Success for the England team depends largely on clubs developing young talent capable of competing with the rest of the world, and so far the progress has been slow. In the United States and Scandinavia, professional women's clubs are commonplace, but in England the only professional club, Fulham, kept their professional status for only three years due to financial constraints and in 2006 were dissolved by their more famous parent club and forced to reform as an independent team. While many talented young English players have benefited from spells in the US, and there are a number of national coaching initiatives under way, it will take some time before a women's team emulates the men's achievements of 1966.

1992-99

All-seater stadia set the stage for English football's top flight to reinvent itself completely. In 1992, leading clubs broke away to form the Premier League. This drove a wedge between the old Football League and the top division and paved the way for a lucrative new Sky TV deal which guaranteed the richest clubs an even greater share of the profits, but took live football away from terrestrial television for the first time since the early 1980s.

The Champions League also changed the landscape, spelling an end for the traditional European Cup and increasing the number of matches the top clubs would play against continental opposition. Manchester United dominated the decade under Sir Alex Ferguson, and ended it by becoming the first English club ever to win the treble of league, FA Cup and European Cup in the same season.

David Beckham established himself as one of the key stars for both United and England, and also eclipsed even George Best as a footballing superstar off the pitch. Yet Beckham ended the decade on a sour note, too, having been sent off as England crashed out of another World Cup finals. He would part company with United in the new millennium, and their dominance would also end as a new English superpower arrived....

EVENTS

1992:
Sky TV

They called it 'a whole new ball game', and while a change in broadcaster might not seem like such a revolutionary event, Sky's involvement in top-flight football heralded a sea change in the game's fortunes. Rupert Murdoch-owned BskyB paid more than £300 million over five years to buy the rights to show live matches. This was a deal warmly welcomed by clubs who had grown tired of the perceived monopoly on television coverage (and revenue) by the larger teams such as Arsenal and Liverpool when ITV showed matches. Sky would show more live matches, spreading the money more evenly around clubs (though not lower division clubs), but the deal also meant fans would have to pay for satellite equipment and subscriptions or view matches from pubs, as terrestrial television was restricted to highlights.

The deal coincided with the start of the Premier League, which had seen the leading 20 First Division clubs 'break away' to form a new league. Although it was still administrated by the FA, and promotion and relegation issues would effectively be the same as before, the Premier League was free to negotiate its own sponsorship, commercial deals and television rights away from the Football League. While Sky's coverage was slick and popular with fans who could afford it, and the Premier League's marketing brought more fans to better stadiums, many believe it marked the start of traditional working-class supporters being priced out of the game for good.

Sky Sports' outside broadcast studio. Sky's involvement in the football franchise was both a blessing and a curse.

Eric Cantona lifts the Champions League trophy for Manchester United in 1993.

1992:
The Champions League

The European Cup got a radical new makeover at the same time as the English First Division. Out went the old knockout competition, and in came a new format which saw a mix of knockout matches and 'group stages' – mini-leagues which decided who would progress to the next round. The competition was also expanded significantly: whereas previously it had been open only to the champions of each European nation, the newly-named Champions League would be weighted according to the footballing pedigree of each country. This meant that England, Italy and Spain could boast three or four entrants each, whereas smaller nations had only one – and these minnows had to take part in qualifying rounds to earn the right to take on the bigger clubs.

The prime driver in these format changes was money: the big clubs wanted to play more frequent prestigious matches against top opposition, and the league format meant their European interest did not end after one defeat. UEFA was keen to appease the increasingly powerful clubs, fearing a breakaway European Super League which would end its power for good. Arsenal competed in the first Champions League but did not make it to the group stage: it would be seven years before an English team won the new competition.

FA CUP WINNERS

1992:	Liverpool 2-0 Sunderland
1993:	Arsenal 1-1 Sheffield Wednesday Replay: Arsenal 2-1 Sheffield Wednesday
1994:	Manchester United 4-0 Chelsea
1995:	Everton 1-0 Manchester United
1996:	Manchester United 1-0 Liverpool
1997:	Chelsea 2-0 Middlesborough
1998:	Arsenal 2-0 Newcastle United
1999:	Manchester United 2-0 Newcastle United

1993:
The Women's Football Association

With the women's game increasing in popularity, the Football Association stepped in to take over the running of the Women's Premier League and the Women's FA Cup, administering them in the same way as the men's game and giving them the benefit of professional marketing expertise to attract larger crowds. Arsenal won the league eight times in the next 13 years, as well as the FA Cup seven times, to become the dominant team in the game. Participation also increased: between 1992 and 2002, the number of women playing the game rose fivefold to more than 60,000 nationally, making it the most popular sport for women to take part in.

It is predicted that, as more girls play the game at school, the number of female footballers at all levels could make the number of male players by 2014. Even so, crowds remain small and professional status is a long way off as sponsorship and infrastructure are slow to arrive: media coverage is slowly increasing, and highlights shows on terrestrial television offer hope of a big future for the women's game.

1999:
Millennium Stadium Opens

The opening of a massive new stadium in Wales was to prove timely for English football. The Millennium Stadium in Cardiff could hold 74,500, making it one of Britain's largest, and it featured the world's biggest retractable roof. It is best known for hosting Welsh rugby internationals, but the Welsh national football team also play there, first appearing in the ground when they drew a then-record crowd of 66,000 as they faced Finland in 2000. When Wembley Stadium was closed for refurbishment at the end of 2000, all major cup finals – including the FA Cup, League Cup and all divisional play-off finals – moved to Cardiff until the new Wembley was ready, while the England national team played at venues including Old Trafford, St James' Park and Anfield.

Cardiff's Millennium Stadium proved timely in light of Wembley's rebuild.

PLAYERS

Tony Adams (b. 1966)

(P: Arsenal, England; M: Wycombe Wanderers)

The ultimate rugged, no-nonsense centre-half, Tony Adams won acclaim for his personal battles as well as those he won on the pitch. He played more than 500 league games in 18 years with Arsenal, first appearing as a 17-year-old in 1984 and making his England debut in 1987 (he went on to win 66 caps). He was pilloried as a 'donkey' by fans after a series of poor performances in the 1988 European Championships, but came back stronger and the following season led the club to the First Division title. In the 1990s, he fought alcoholism publicly but rebuilt his career successfully and captained Arsenal to two doubles, in 1998 and 2002, before retiring.

David Beckham (b. 1975)

(Manchester United, Real Madrid, England)

Not since George Best has a British footballer become as famous outside the game as David Beckham. When he first became a Manchester United regular in 1994, he was noticed for his looks as much as his playing ability, and his later marriage to Spice Girl Victoria Adams elevated him to superstar status, generating him millions in endorsements. On the pitch, Beckham was a brilliant passer and crosser of the ball, and became famous for his deadly free kicks. His dismissal in the 1998 World Cup was infamous, but he inspired United to the 1999 treble and became England

Tony Adams overcame a series of demons both on and off the pitch.

captain under Sven-Göran Eriksson. Beckham's growing rift with Sir Alex Ferguson saw him leave United for Real Madrid in 2003, but he continued to be a key figure for his country until he was dropped by Eriksson's replacement, Steve McLaren, in 2006.

Dennis Bergkamp (b. 1969)

(Ajax, Inter Milan, Arsenal, Netherlands)

Dennis Bergkamp is the most celebrated foreign player ever to appear in the English game, and his arrival at Arsenal in 1995 was a significant step towards making the Premier League the most exciting in the world. The Dutchman was already one of the game's most accomplished forwards: technically brilliant, fleet-footed and a scorer of spectacular goals. At Highbury, the team was built around his abilities and he was adored by the crowd as the key player in the club's renaissance in the late 1990s. His last game in professional football was Arsenal's last at Highbury, in May 2006.

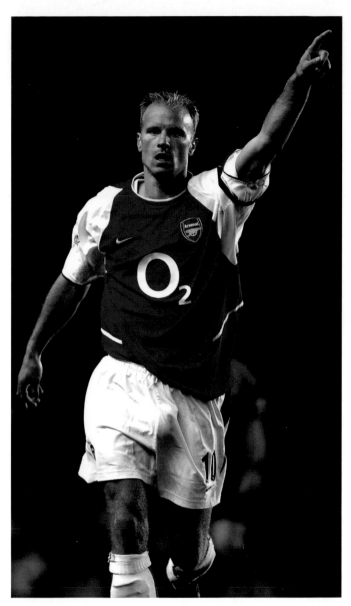

Above: Dutch forward Dennis Bergkamp brought his talents to teams in Holland, Italy and England.

Left: David Beckham is the epitome of a footballing superstar.

FOOTBALL WRITERS' ASSOCIATION FOOTBALLER OF THE YEAR

1992:	Gary Lineker	Tottenham Hotspur
1993:	Chris Waddle	Sheffield Wednesday
1994:	Alan Shearer	Blackburn Rovers
1995:	Jürgen Klinsman	Tottenham Hotspur
1996:	Eric Cantona	Manchester United
1997:	Gianfranco Zola	Chelsea
1998:	Dennis Bergkamp	Arsenal
1999:	David Ginola	Tottenham Hotspur

Sol Campbell (b. 1974)

(Tottenham, Arsenal, Portsmouth, England)

Sol Campbell's 2001 move from Tottenham to Arsenal became one of the most controversial transfers English football has ever seen. Campbell had come through the ranks at White Hart Lane to become a regular with Spurs and England, but his decision to join the club's bitter rivals on a free transfer under the Bosman ruling led to a hate campaign from Tottenham

supporters, who have still never forgiven him. Campbell won the double in his first season at Highbury, and was a defensive rock for club and country before he lost his Arsenal place after missing several days' training for 'personal reasons'. He left in 2006 to join Portsmouth.

Eric Cantona (b. 1966)

(Auxerre, Marseille, Bordeaux, Montpellier, Nimes, Leeds United, Manchester United, France)

Poet, philosopher, footballing genius and violent brawler: Eric Cantona kept the English public mesmerised for five whirlwind years after crossing the Channel in 1992. He was already infamous in his native France, having insulted both the national coach and the FA before retiring from the game at the age of 25. In England, he joined Leeds and inspired them to the league title before making the short journey to Old Trafford and becoming a Manchester United legend. Cantona's skills, and the ease with which he beat defenders, were breathtaking, but his unpredictability was just as captivating. He made the front pages in January 1995 when he kung fu-kicked a supporter who had mocked him following a red card at Crystal Palace. He was banned for nine months, but came back to enjoy his best season, inspiring United to the 1996 double and scoring the winning goal in the FA Cup final against Liverpool. A year later, he shocked the game by announcing his retirement, aged 30.

Fiery French footballer Eric Cantona.

Sir Alex Ferguson (b. 1941)

(P: Queens Park, St Johnstone, Dunfermline, Rangers, Falkirk, Ayr United; M: East Stirling, St Mirren, Aberdeen, Scotland, Manchester United)

Though his appointment at Manchester United took some by surprise, Alex Ferguson already had a fine pedigree in Scotland, having transformed Aberdeen from also-rans into European Cup Winners' Cup victors. At Old Trafford, he had to overhaul a club which had become bogged down in the past, with many ageing stars, and he put the emphasis on developing an excellent youth system which would flourish in the 1990s and bring him eight league titles as well as the famous treble of league, FA Cup and European Cup in 1999. Ferguson's disciplinary style (his angry rants at players are known as the 'hairdryer treatment') have led to fall-outs with big names including David Beckham, but have made him one of the game's most successful domestic bosses ever.

The best-known manager in England, Alex Ferguson.

Andy Cole has impressed for Man U, although rarely for England.

Andy Cole (b. 1971)

(Arsenal, Bristol City, Newcastle, Manchester United, Blackburn Rovers, Fulham, Portsmouth, England)

Though he has endured periods of criticism and never made the grade with the national team, Andy Cole is one of the most consistently prolific goalscorers of the modern era. He was allowed to leave by Arsenal as a youngster, but after a brilliant season with Bristol City he was picked up by Kevin Keegan's Newcastle, scoring a club record 41 goals during the 1992/93 campaign. That led to him joining Manchester United for more than £37 million in 1994, and at Old Trafford his strike rate of a goal every other game made him one of the club's deadliest-ever strikers, as he won four Premiership titles in five years.

Paul Gascoigne's career ended in injury and ignominy.

Paul Gascoigne (b. 1967)

(Newcastle, Tottenham, Lazio, Rangers, Middlesbrough, Everton, Burnley, Boston United, England)

Uniquely gifted – as fine a dribbler as Stanley Matthews and a brilliantly creative midfielder – Paul Gascoigne is also known for the self-destructive streak and spate of injuries which arguably stopped him realising his full potential. Having come through the ranks with his native Newcastle, Gascoigne joined Terry Venables' Tottenham and was brilliant in the 1989/90 season, which culminated in his famous tears in the World Cup semi-final. Gascoigne was the hottest property in the game, but the following year he ruptured cruciate ligaments during a wild challenge in the FA Cup final, and some argue he was never the same player again.

He enjoyed little success with Lazio in Italy (though he delighted fans with his belching antics, false breasts and sense of fun), but won three titles at Glasgow Rangers (enjoying fine form in England's Euro 96 campaign, including a famous goal against Scotland). Shorter spells at Middlesbrough and Everton followed, as his drink and psychological problems became well-documented, and lack of form and fitness eventually ended his career on an unsatisfactory note.

Ryan Giggs (b. 1973)

(Manchester United, Wales)

A throwback to the days of skilful, super-quick wingers, Ryan Giggs is an all-time Manchester United great. He scored the winner in the Manchester derby on his full United debut in 1991 and was soon being compared to George Best. He kept a lower profile than team-mate

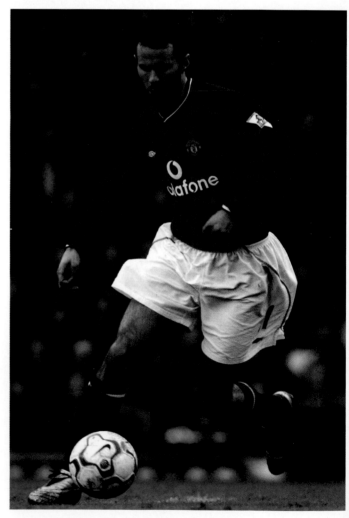

Wales and Manchester United star Ryan Giggs.

Hughes had a long playing career before finding success as a manager.

Roy Keane (b. 1971)

(P: Nottingham Forest, Manchester United, Celtic, Ireland; M: Sunderland)

Known for his fiery temper and controversial bust-ups, Roy Keane was one of the hardest-working and most effective midfielders of his generation. He was spotted by Nottingham Forest in his native Ireland and moulded by Brian Clough into a superb all-round midfield dynamo before joining Manchester United for a then record £3.75 million in 1993. He was the heartbeat of Alex Ferguson's team for more than a decade, winning seven league titles in the process, although he was suspended for the 1999 European Cup final. He left United under a cloud in 2005, but his most controversial moment had occurred in 2002, when he left the Ireland World Cup squad in Japan after an argument with manager Mick McCarthy.

Irish powerhouse Roy Keane.

David Beckham, but was just as effective, rampaging down the left wing and setting up many vital goals as United dominated the 1990s. His own FA Cup semi-final goal against Arsenal in 1999 is regarded as one of the best the competition has ever seen. Though he grew up in England, Giggs is proudly Welsh and, like Best, missed out on the chance of making it to a major international tournament despite his superstar status.

Mark Hughes (b. 1963)

(P: Manchester United, Barcelona, Bayern Munich, Chelsea, Southampton, Everton, Blackburn, Wales; M: Wales, Blackburn)

Mark Hughes came through the ranks at Old Trafford to establish himself as a powerful goal scorer, before being sold to Terry Venables' Barcelona in 1986. He did not hit it off with strike partner Gary Lineker in Spain, and returned to Old Trafford under Alex Ferguson, winning two league titles and two FA Cups. He also won the cup after leaving for Chelsea and went on to appear for Everton and Blackburn before enjoying considerable success as Wales manager, taking his country agonisingly close to the Euro 2004 finals.

Jurgen Klinsmann was popular as a Spurs player, but that changed when he donned the German jersey.

Jurgen Klinsmann (b. 1964)

(P: Stuttgart Kickers, Stuttgart, Inter Milan, Monaco, Tottenham, Bayern Munich, Sampdoria; M: Germany)

One of Germany's greatest-ever players, Jurgen Klinsmann was a colourful and popular figure in the Premier League during two spells with Tottenham. He first joined in 1994, and mocked the reputation the press had given him as a 'diver' by diving headlong into the turf after scoring his first goal for the club. Tottenham finished seventh that year, but a misunderstanding over the length of Klinsmann's contract led to chairman Alan Sugar famously declaring he would not even wash his car with the player's shirt. Nonetheless, Klinsmann returned in 1996 and scored nine goals to help Spurs beat the drop.

Manchester United veteran Gary Neville.

Gary Neville (b. 1975)

(Manchester United, England)

Gary Neville has been a consistent unsung hero of Manchester United's achievements under Sir Alex Ferguson. He first emerged in 1992 (followed by younger brother Phil) and was soon the club's regular right-back,

a mainstay of their excellent late 1990s teams and captain since 2005, passing the 500-game mark for United in 2006. He is also heading towards 100 England caps, and appeared for his country in Euro 96 and 2002, as well as the 1998 and 2006 World Cups.

Martin O'Neill (b. 1952)

(P: Nottingham Forest, Norwich City, Manchester City, Notts County, Northern Ireland; M: Wycombe Wanderers, Norwich City, Leicester City, Celtic, Aston Villa)

Martin O'Neill learned the art of management from Brian Clough as part of the Nottingham Forest side which won the European Cup twice. He also appeared for Northern Ireland in their famous 1982 World Cup victory over Spain, and after entering the dugout took Wycombe Wanderers into the league for the first time. He then took Leicester City to the Premiership and into Europe before leaving to join Celtic, where he became famed for his enthusiasm and motivational skills. Overlooked for the England job in 2006, he is now reshaping Aston Villa to challenge for major honours.

Marc Overmars (b. 1973)

(Go Ahead Eagles, Willem II, Ajax, Arsenal, Barcelona, Netherlands)

Marc Overmars' move to Arsenal in the summer of 1997 was the final ingredient in Arsène Wenger's plan to wrestle the championship from Alex Ferguson's Manchester United. The flying Dutch winger, who terrified defenders with his pace, inspired the Gunners to the double in his first season. He played 125 games for Arsenal and starred for club and country alongside Dennis Bergkamp, but left in 2000 for a largely unhappy spell with Barcelona.

Stuart Pearce (b. 1962)

(P: Coventry, Nottingham Forest, Newcastle, West Ham, Manchester City, England; P&M: Nottingham Forest; M: Manchester City)

Immediately recognisable, and respected throughout the game, Stuart Pearce was known as 'Psycho' for his combative displays, but despite a hard-man reputation was a fair player and a skilful overlapping left-back. Feared for his thunderbolt shot and crunching tackles, Pearce entered the game late but became a favourite at

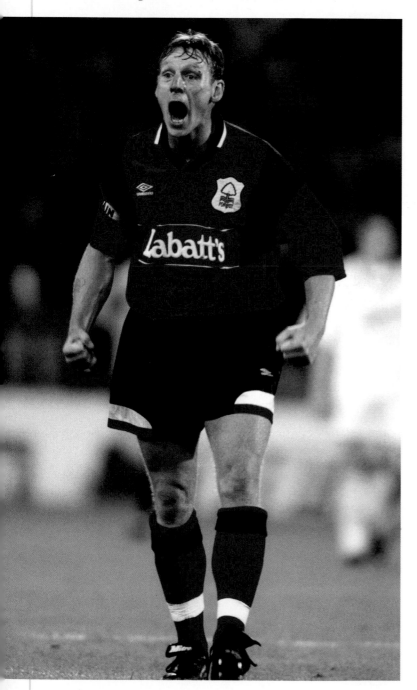

Stuart Pearce demonstrates why his nickname was Psycho.

Nottingham Forest under Brian Clough, and was even player-manager of the club for a while. He is best remembered for his time in the national team: his missed penalty in the 1990 World Cup helped send England home, but at Euro 96 he volunteered to take part in a shoot-out again and celebrated wildly when his spot-kick was successful against Spain.

Peter Schmeichel (b. 1963)

(Brondby, Manchester United, Sporting Lisbon, Aston Villa, Manchester City, Denmark)

Regarded by many as the greatest goalkeeper of all-time, Manchester United's many honours of the 1990s – including the 1999 treble – would have been impossible without Peter Schmeichel, a man-mountain between the posts. Schmeichel was agile, fearless and unbeatable in the air. He was virtually unknown in England when Alex Ferguson brought him to Old Trafford in 1991, but his ability was immediately obvious and his finest hour came when he lifted the 1999 European Cup as captain. He was also the mainstay of the Denmark team who were the shock winners of the 1992 European Championships.

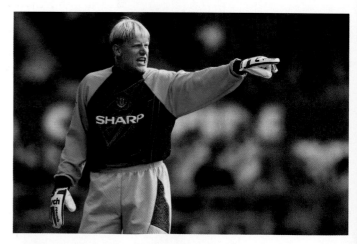

England players' nemesis Peter Schmeichel.

Paul Scholes (b. 1974)

(Manchester United, England)

Though he shirks the limelight which many of his Manchester United team-mates have enjoyed, Paul Scholes has been a vital cog in the club's success and is one of Alex Ferguson's most highly rated players. He emerged in 1994, but was not a United regular until 1997, when

England stalwart Paul Scholes shows his acrobatic ability.

Ferguson reshaped the team to accommodate his talents. Scholes is at his best as an attacking midfielder, making well-timed runs into the box – he has an excellent strike rate for someone who plays relatively deep. He retired from international football in 2004 after winning 66 caps.

David Seaman (b. 1963)

(Peterborough, Birmingham, QPR, Arsenal, Manchester City, England)

In 1990, George Graham needed a new goalkeeper to cement the rock-solid defence he was building at Arsenal. He turned to 26-year-old David Seaman, in a move which surprised many but was to turn out to be a master-stroke. Seaman conceded only 18 goals during the whole of the 1990/91 season as Arsenal won the championship, and he became one of the finest goalkeepers in the country. He took over as first-choice England stopper in 1994 and retained this role until the 2002 World Cup, when his high-profile error in letting in a 40-yard Ronaldinho free-kick was a career low-point.

David Seaman, whose large gloves and ponytail made him a distinctive figure in the England goalmouth.

Alan Shearer (b. 1970)

(Southampton, Blackburn, Newcastle United, England)

One of the most prolific English strikers ever, Alan Shearer's clean-cut reputation and incredible consistency make him an icon for a generation of players. The Tyneside-born goalscorer was rejected by Newcastle as a boy, and instead began his career at Southampton, scoring a hat-trick on his full debut against Arsenal, as a 17-year-old. He won the league with Blackburn in 1992, before fulfilling a dream by joining Newcastle for a world record £15 million. He was unable to win a major title in 10 years at St James' Park, but was adored by the Geordie public for his 206 goals for the club – bettering Jackie Milburn's record. He also scored 30 times in 63 games for England before retiring from international football in 2000.

Terry Venables – better as manager than player.

Terry Venables (b. 1943)

(P: Chelsea, Tottenham, QPR, Crystal Palace, England; M: Crystal Palace, QPR, Barcelona, Tottenham, England, Portsmouth, Australia, Leeds United)

A capable player with two England caps, Terry 'El Tel' Venables' greatest achievements were as a manager. He became a fans' favourite while England boss during Euro 96, known for his straightforward style on the pitch and straight talking off it, though England failed to win the tournament. His first managerial achievement was taking Crystal Palace to fifth in the old First Division. He failed in his aim to make the Eagles the 'Team of the Eighties' but won a number of honours with Barcelona and later built an entertaining Tottenham team before off-the-field business activities began to overshadow his managerial career.

Sheringham (above) and Shearer (right) formed a dynamic duo.

Teddy Sheringham (b. 1966)

(Millwall, Nottingham Forest, Tottenham, Manchester United, Portsmouth, West Ham, England)

Few were surprised by Teddy Sheringham's decision to carry on as a Premiership player when he turned 40: while he was always short of pace, the razor-sharp instincts and intelligent team-play which marked the striker's 20-year career at the top of the game were undiminished. Sheringham made his name with Tottenham, but won his first major honours during Manchester United's treble year of 1999, including a vital goal in the European Cup final. He formed a deadly partnership with Alan Shearer at international level, winning 51 England caps in all.

THE PFA PLAYERS' PLAYER OF THE YEAR

1992:	Gary Pallister	Manchester United
1993:	Paul McGrath	Aston Villa
1994:	Eric Cantona	Manchester United
1995:	Alan Shearer	Blackburn Rovers
1996:	Les Ferdinand	Newcastle United
1997:	Alan Shearer	Newcastle United
1998:	Dennis Bergkamp	Arsenal
1999:	David Ginola	Tottenham Hotspur

Arsenal engine room Patrick Vieira.

Patrick Vieira (b. 1976)

(Cannes, AC Milan, Arsenal, Juventus, Inter Milan, France)

Patrick Vieira was languishing in Milan's reserves when Arsène Wenger made him his first signing on taking over at Arsenal in 1996. Many questioned the move, but the tough-tackling midfielder soon became the team's engine room and won three league titles, becoming captain following Tony Adams' retirement in 2002. Vieira also won the 1998 World Cup and 2000 European Championship with France, but he was a controversial figure in the domestic game, often clashing with referees and opponents (including Roy Keane) and being sent off 10 times for the Gunners.

Arsène Wenger (b. 1949)

(P: Strasbourg; M: Nancy, Monaco, Grampus Eight (Japan), Arsenal)

Arsène Wenger was virtually unknown in England when he was appointed Arsenal manager in 1996. He had achieved success in France with Monaco, but had spent the previous 18 months in Japan. He quickly rebuilt the ailing Gunners, however, bringing in players (many of them French) with a desire to succeed and considerable flair, among them Patrick Vieira and Thierry Henry – both plucked from Italian clubs' reserve teams. Wenger's meticulous planning led Arsenal to 1998 and 2002 league and FA Cup doubles, and they went the entire 2003/04 season without defeat. He is one of the country's most respected managers, and enjoys a high-profile rivalry with Sir Alex Ferguson.

Dwight Yorke left his native Trinidad to become one of the best strikers in the Premiership.

Dwight Yorke (b. 1971)

(Aston Villa, Manchester United, Blackburn Rovers, Birmingham City, Sydney FC (Australia), Sunderland, Trinidad & Tobago)

Former England manager Graham Taylor discovered Dwight Yorke when Aston Villa toured the West Indies in 1989; he immediately took the Trinidadian teenager to Villa Park, and over the next nine seasons Yorke was to become one of the best strikers in the Premiership. He joined Manchester United in 1998 and his partnership with Andy Cole was a key factor in the treble-winning season of 1998/99. In 2006, Yorke appeared in the World Cup finals with his country, and later joined ex-team-mate Roy Keane at Sunderland.

Gianfranco Zola (b. 1966)

(Nuorese, Turris, Napoli, Parma, Chelsea, Calgliari, Italy)

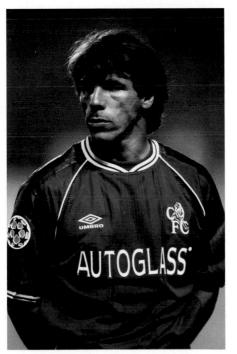

Chelsea's capture of Gianfranco Zola in 1996 was one of the Premiership's biggest coups, and he came to be widely admired outside of Stamford Bridge for his enthusiasm and happy-go-lucky approach to the game, as well as his notable skills. Zola had been seen as the new Diego Maradona while starring for Napoli, and in London he became known for his excellent goals, including one as Chelsea won the Cup Winners' Cup in 1998 to end a long wait for a European trophy. He returned to his native Sardinia in 2003 to spend his last two seasons with Calgliari.

Much-loved Gianfranco Zola.

MATCHES

Liverpool 4-3 Newcastle United

Premiership, Anfield, 10 March 1996

Liverpool: (Man. Roy Evans) James, Kvarme, McAteer, Wright, McManaman, Fowler, Barnes, Redknapp, Berger, Bjornebye, Matteo

Newcastle United: (Man. Kevin Keegan) Hislop, Barton, Peacock, Elliott, Albert, Watson, Batty, Clark (Ginola), Asprilla, Gillespie, Beardsley (Ferdinand (Crawford))

Scorers: Liverpool: McManaman 29, Berger 30, Fowler 42, 90; Newcastle: Gillespie 71, Asprilla 87, Barton 88

Liverpool wins the FA Carling Premiership, March 1996.

Voted the greatest match in Premiership history, Newcastle's defeat at Anfield also marked the beginning of the end for their title hopes under Kevin Keegan. The Magpies were leading Manchester United in the race for the championship, but they were 3-0 down at half-time and looked dead and buried. Their comeback began when Keith Gillespie scored, and with three minutes left Faustino Asprilla and Warren Barton both found the net in quick succession to level the match. Incredibly, Liverpool had the last laugh in a breathless finale, Robbie Fowler netting his second of the match right at the death. Newcastle won only four of their last 10 matches and surrendered the title to Alex Ferguson's men.

England 4-1 Holland
European Championship Finals, Wembley, 18 June 1996

England: (Man. Terry Venables) Seaman, G. Neville, Pearce, Ince (Platt), Southgate, Adams, Anderton, Gascoigne, Shearer (Fowler), Sheringham (Barmby), McManaman

Holland: (Man. Guus Hiddink) Van der Sar, Reiziger, Blind, Seedorf, R. de Boer (Kluivert), Bergkamp, Hoekstra (Cocu), Winter, Witschge (de Kock), Bogarde, Cruyff

Scorers: England: Shearer 23 (pen), 57, Sheringham 51, 62; Holland: Kluivert 78

Stuart Pearce tackles Jordi Cruyff at Wembley, June 1996.

FOOTBALL LEAGUE CHAMPIONS	
1992/93:	Manchester United
1993/94:	Manchester United
1994/95:	Blackburn Rovers
1995/96:	Manchester United
1996/97:	Manchester United
1997/98:	Arsenal
1998/99:	Manchester United
1999/2000:	Manchester United

England's clinical destruction of an excellent Dutch team in the group stages made the country believe the hosts could win Euro 96. With Paul Gascoigne pulling the strings in a vintage performance, the deadly strike duo of Alan Shearer and Teddy Sheringham scored two apiece. The third goal was the best of them all, with Gascoigne rampaging through the defence before laying off to Sheringham, who dummied to shoot before instead playing in Shearer to smash the ball into the top corner. England defeated Spain on penalties in the quarter-finals but once again suffered shoot-out agony in the semi-final against the Germans.

England 2-2 Argentina
World Cup Second Round, Saint Etienne, 30 June 1998

England: (Man. Glenn Hoddle) Seaman, G. Neville, Campbell, Adams, Le Saux (Southgate), Anderton (Batty), Ince, Beckham, Scholes (Merson), Shearer, Owen

Argentina: (Man. Daniel Passarella) Roa, Ayala, Chamot, Vivas, Zanetti, Almeyda, Simeone (Berti), Ortega, Veron, Lopez (Gallardo), Batistuta (Crespo)

Scorers: England: Shearer 10 (pen), Owen 16; Batistuta 5 (pen), Zanetti 45

England had come through a relatively easy group to reach the second round of France 98, but the realisation they would face old foes Argentina in the knockout stage put a dampener on the optimistic travelling support. Things looked bad when a Gabriel Batistuta put the South Americans ahead from the penalty spot, but England were quickly level when Michael Owen went down under the minimum of contact from Roberto Ayala to allow Alan Shearer to slot home the resulting penalty.

David Beckham is sent for an early bath in World Cup '98.

Owen was England's great hope: just 18 and in his first full season with Liverpool, his sensational scoring ability was the talk of the game and he came of age in the 16th minute, setting off on a long run which ended with a powerful finish past goalkeeper Carlos Roa and an ecstatic celebration. Javier Zanetti equalised before the first half was out, and the game then hinged on an incident two minutes into the second half, when a floored David Beckham aimed a kick at Argentina's Diego Simeone. The Inter Milan player undoubtedly over-reacted, but the referee reached for the red card and Beckham's astonishing rise to fame was at an end – he would receive death threats and be vilified by the media in the wake of the sending-off, and would have to wait several years to rebuild his reputation. England hung on manfully to force a penalty shoot-out, but David Batty's spot-kick was saved and they went home to an anti-climax as the hosts won the trophy.

Arsenal 1-2 Manchester United
FA Cup Semi-Final Replay, Villa Park, 14 April 1999

Arsenal: (Man. Arsène Wenger) Seaman, Dixon, Winterburn, Adams, Keown, Vieira, Ljungberg (Overmars), Parlour (Kanu), Petit (Bould), Anelka, Bergkamp

Manchester United: (Man. Alex Ferguson) Schmeichel, G. Neville, P. Neville, Johnsen, Stam, Beckham, Butt, Keane, Blomqvist (Giggs), Solskjaer (Yorke), Sheringham (Scholes)

Scorers: Arsenal: Bergkamp 69; Manchester United: Beckham 17, Giggs 109

With the two clubs locking horns at the top of the table, the rivalry between Arsenal and Manchester United had never been fiercer when they met in the FA Cup semi-final in 1999. The two clubs had been involved in a goalless draw three days earlier, and in the Villa Park replay David Beckham struck first with a sublime long-range goal to put United ahead. Dennis Bergkamp equalised for Arsenal and was then involved in two moments of drama as normal time finished all-square, seeing a goal disallowed in controversial circumstances and having a penalty saved by Peter Schmeichel. Despite having lost Roy Keane after a second yellow card, United dug deep and a Ryan Giggs wonder-goal – as he ran from the halfway line and past three defenders to score – settled the tie. United won the final 2-0 against Newcastle and also pipped Arsenal to the title to complete a miserable season for the Gunners.

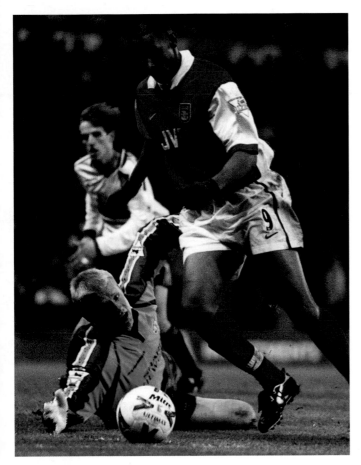

Nicolas Anelka gets one over on Peter Schmeichel, April 1999.

Manchester United 2-1 Bayern Munich
European Cup Final, Barcelona, 26 May 1999

Manchester United: (Man. Alex Ferguson) Schmeichel, G. Neville, Irwin, Johnsen, Stam, Beckham, Butt, Giggs, Blomqvist (Sheringham), Cole (Solskjaer), Yorke

Bayern Munich: (Man. Ottmar Hitzfeld) Kahn, Babbel, Kuffour, Matthaus (Fink), Effenberg, Basler (Salihamidzic), Jeremies, Tarnat, Zickler (Scholl), Linke, Jancker

Scorers: Manchester United: Sheringham 90, Solskjaer 90; Bayern Munich: Basler 6

With the League and FA Cup double already sewn up, Manchester United were on course for an historic treble – never before achieved by an English club

– when they met Bayern Munich in the Nou Camp to contest the European Cup. With talismanic captain Roy Keane suspended, United seemed strangely subdued and they struggled to get back into the game after Mario Basler's goal put the Germans ahead. As the clock wore down, Bayern fans began celebrating victory as Sir Alex Ferguson urged his team on for one final effort. It was to prove the most dramatic conclusion ever to a major final. Twenty seconds into injury time, David Beckham's corner was whipped in with goalkeeper Peter Schmeichel joining every outfield player in the box to contest it. A scramble developed and Teddy Sheringham smashed the ball home. Ninety seconds later, another Beckham corner was met by Sheringham's head and nodded on for fellow substitute Ole Gunnar Solskjaer to finish from close range. Bayern were shattered, and millions were stunned as they watched the events unfold on television. Stand-in skipper Schmeichel lifted the trophy in an amazing victory not just for United, but for the entire country.

The Treble-winning Manchester United team returns home.

Manchester United 1993–2003
Alex Ferguson

Key Players: David Beckham (midfielder), Roy Keane (midfielder), Peter Schmeichel (goalkeeper)

Trophies: Premiership 1993, 1994, 1996, 1997, 1999, 2000, 2001, 2003; FA Cup 1994, 1996, 1999; European Cup 1999

Sir Alex Ferguson's success at Manchester United is an abject lesson in patience. When the Scotsman was appointed in 1986, there were many who believed he would struggle to turn around a club which had spent two decades under-achieving since the glories of the Matt Busby era.

Back From The Brink

Although United showed some improvement after Ferguson's arrival, by January 1990 they were at the wrong

end of the table and the manager had already endured calls for his head after a 5-1 derby thrashing at Manchester City's hands. Local papers were predicting Ferguson was 90 minutes away from the sack when the team faced favourites Nottingham Forest in the third round of the FA Cup, but a Mark Robins goal handed United the win and by eventually winning the cup and staying up, Ferguson was given the time he needed to rebuild the club. Behind the scenes, he had given Old Trafford the best scouting network in Britain and brought in coaches who would develop world-class youngsters to their full potential. The first such player, Ryan Giggs, would be a regular as United won their first league title for 26 long years, in 1993.

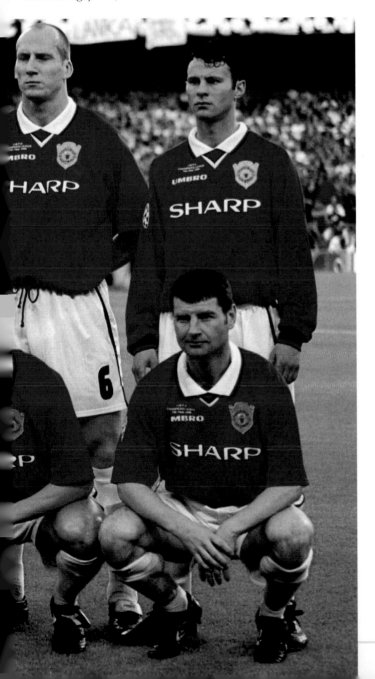

New Kids On The Block

Ferguson was still relying on old hands like Steve Bruce and Brian McClair, but had brought in giant goalkeeper Peter Schmeichel to help improve United's defensive record and had recruited nomadic French genius Eric Cantona to provide flair. Ferguson needed a midfield general and signed Roy Keane that summer: the double followed. A number of players, including Mark Hughes, Bryan Robson and Paul Ince, had moved on but by 1996, United's new crop of youngsters were ready for the first team: David Beckham, Nicky Butt, Paul Scholes and the Neville brothers all made an immediate impact as the team took the double again. The manager was moulding his players into a system, always replacing like with like and ensuring no individual could become bigger than the club – as Beckham was to find out.

Treble-Tastic

With Andy Cole and Dwight Yorke forming a potent partnership, United went one better with the 1999 treble, and would win the title three more times up to 2003, as they showed their dominance over new foes Arsenal (this rivalry would growing increasingly bitter, culminating in the so-called 'Battle of the Buffet' in 2004, when Arsenal players allegedly threw food at United, and Wenger and Ferguson fought in the tunnel). The 2003 title was secured despite Arsenal leading the race by 18 points at one point: Ferguson's mind games, and United's determination, ate into that lead and showed why their manager was the greatest of the era.

The unstoppable Manchester team that brought home the Treble.

FOOTBALL LEAGUE CUP WINNERS

1992:	Manchester United 1-0 Nottingham Forest
1993:	Arsenal 2-1 Sheffield Wednesday
1994:	Aston Villa 3-1 Manchester United
1995:	Liverpool 2-1 Bolton Wanderers
1996:	Aston Villa 3-0 Leeds United
1997:	Leicester City 1-1 Middlesborough
	Replay: Leicester City 1-0 Middlesborough
1998:	Chelsea 2-0 Middlesborough
1999:	Tottenham Hotspur 1-0 Leicester City

FEATURES

The Role Of The Media

For most of the twentieth century, the relationship between football and the mass media was fairly cosy – some would say too cosy. Newspapers restricted themselves to reporting matter-of-fact happenings and detailing matches in a methodical, impartial way, but genuine analysis was hard to come by. Many significant events which should have been exposed (including the match-fixing scandal of 1964, which saw eight players jailed) were conveniently swept under the carpet. Television was restricted to straightforward commentary of carefully selected highlights.

Ravaged By The Red Tops

By the late 1980s, the tabloids were changing. Kelvin MacKenzie's *Sun*, and others, had realised that fans were fascinated by transfer gossip, scandals and details of players' lifestyles, and began to reflect this in their coverage. Players' wages were the subject of intense speculation, as were potential moves and any perceived dressing-room bust-ups. More significantly, newspapers began to editorialise about players' and managers' abilities, and England managers were seen as fair game by the press. Bobby Robson was the first to face such ire, with one headline demanding 'In the name of God, go!' after England's poor performance in the 1988 European

Fans began to form their opinions based on what they read in the newspapers, and the media could make or break a footballing career.

England manager Graham Taylor leaves the field after the World Cup qualifier against Holland.

Championships. Robson's replacement, Graham Taylor, was the subject of even more intense pressure as England crashed out of the 1992 European finals: *The Sun* ran the headline 'Swedes 2 Turnips 1' following the defeat to the hosts and superimposed his head onto a turnip to demand his sacking. He returned home to a media frenzy and was hounded for some time by journalists and photographers.

Bobby Robson.

Far From Satisfactory

As players and their agents became more astute, however, they began to use the press to their advantage, being photographed wearing branded clothes to appease their sponsors, boosting their profiles by appearing at showbiz events or 'planting' stories which were designed to earn lucrative transfers or pay rises. Meanwhile, Sky's entry into the television market led to a deeper analysis of the game, both tactically (as Andy Gray used new technological tools to highlight teams' shortcomings) and controversially (as incidents were replayed and debated endlessly by pundits). Many people believe match officials now need access to television replays during matches, to prevent their mistakes being highlighted to the nation afterwards. Managers started to clash with television commentators as frequently as they did journalists, with the BBC earning a ban from Old Trafford press conferences from Alex Ferguson after asking him about a Roy Keane sending-off in 1995. The relationship between football and the media remains mutually beneficial, but is by no means happy.

Football In The Mass Media

As football emerged from the unpleasant 1980s and became increasingly fashionable, so it began to be reflected in wider culture.

Limited Coverage

There had been surprisingly little crossover into the mass media before this point: for instance, few major films had been based around the game save for the likes of *Escape To Victory* (a 1981 film set in a prisoner-of-war camp in which an Allied team must play their captors, featuring cameos from Pele, Bobby Moore and members of the Ipswich Town team), and books were largely bland autobiographies which gave little insight into players' lives off the pitch (Hunter Davies' behind-the-scenes book on Tottenham's 1961 double-winning team, *The Glory Game*, being a notable exception).

Fever Pitch

As broadsheets began to devote greater coverage to more lyrical and intelligent analysis of all facets of the game, it was inevitable the literary world would follow suit, and in

Escape to Victory, starring Michael Caine, was one of the few films to have a footballing theme prior to the mid-1990s.

Footballers' Wives brought the WAGs into the public eye.

1992 Nick Hornby's debut novel, *Fever Pitch*, was credited with creating a genre of intelligent football literature dealing with fans' responses to the game. The book followed an Arsenal supporter's life during the 1988/89 championship-winning season; it became a successful film five years later, but others who tried to follow Hornby's formula met with mixed success. A number of glossy adult football magazines also appeared around this time (the only previous football publications, *Shoot!* and *Match*, having been aimed at children), although only one, *FourFourTwo*, is still being published today.

Balls On The Screen

Hollywood woke up to the game in 2002 as *Bend It Like Beckham* – which told of a young British girl's struggle to persuade her Indian parents to allow her to play football – gained international success. The crossover continued into television, with Sky launching *Dream Team* – a soap opera based around a football club – and the later success of *Footballer's Wives*, a tongue-in-cheek look at players' lifestyles. Meanwhile, newspaper coverage of the game reached saturation point, with frequent supplements giving details of every match and thousands of websites launching during the 1990s devoted to every conceivable area of interest: clubs jumped on this bandwagon by selling tickets and merchandise through their own sites.

Kiss-And-Tell

Players understood the need to make controversial comments or offer revelations in order to make their

autobiographies successful, which led to the media furore surrounding Roy Keane (who admitted in print deliberately injuring Manchester City's Alf Inge Haaland in revenge for a previous incident).

Bend it Like Beckham opened up the game to a new – female – fanbase.

2000 AND BEYOND

By 2003, the Premiership had changed dramatically, when Russian billionaire Roman Abramovich bought Chelsea for £60 million and began spending huge sums on players' wages and transfer fees. The likes of Andriy Shevchenko and Ashley Cole were attracted to Stamford Bridge over the next few seasons as Chelsea were transformed from also-rans into Premiership winners under Jose Mourinho's stewardship, but Abramovich's arrival had a significant knock-on effect for the English game as a whole.

Firstly, it confirmed the Premiership as the most attractive league for the world's best talent, cementing a reputation which had already attracted Cantona, Zola and others to these shores. Secondly, it sent transfer fees across the globe, but particularly in England, into overdrive. And thirdly, it ended a long run of power-sharing between Arsenal and Manchester United, although the Londoners were still in the ascendancy in 2004, going an entire season unbeaten to match Preston's nineteenth-century achievements.

One prize Abramovich's money could not immediately buy was the Champions League, and this was won in 2005 by Liverpool, in circumstances every bit as dramatic as Manchester United's last-gasp 1999 victory.

EVENTS

2000:
Wembley Stadium Closes

After 77 years as the home of English football, Wembley was closed in 2000 to undergo a massive refurbishment to turn it into a twenty-first century stadium. Although the hallowed turf had stayed intact since 1923, the stadium around it had gradually decayed and spectators were demanding more legroom and better facilities of the kind they found elsewhere in the game.

The famous twin towers of Wembley stadium during the demolition of this English icon.

Bulldozers moved in to demolish Wembley's famous Twin Towers in 2001, to be replaced with a giant arch which would form the largest single-span roof structure in the world. Wembley, when rebuilt, would boast 90,000 seats, making it the largest all-seater football ground in the world, along with a part-retractable roof cover. Delays and disputes meant an opening date for the new Wembley was continually being put back, and in the meantime the England team toured top-flight grounds, while cup finals and play-offs went to the Millennium Stadium in Cardiff.

2002:
ITV Digital Crash

The collapse of digital terrestrial television channel ITV Digital (formerly ONDigital) hit Football League clubs hard. The fledgling broadcaster had bought the rights to screen matches from outside the Premiership in 2001, paying £315 million for a three-year contract in what many experts felt was a poor deal for ITV. A year later, the channel was losing around £1 million a day, and its gamble on football – which it hoped would draw huge audiences to buy its set-top boxes and pay subscription fees to watch its channels – was backfiring, with audiences frequently smaller than the attendance at the match itself (several matches had official viewing figures of zero because too few people were tuning in to be recorded).

ITV Digital announced it was unable to pay the remaining £180 million it owed under the contract; the Football League offered a compromise deal involving paying £90 million up front and the rest in instalments, but ITV insisted it could afford no more than £50 million. No deal was reached, and the League eventually took ITV to court, losing the case and any future payments in the process. Meanwhile, clubs were plunged into crisis: those in the First Division expected £3 million per season, which they had budgeted for and in some cases spent but was now being taken from them. Even those in the basement division were due £300,000 per season from ITV – up to 20 per cent of their overall income.

Hundreds of players were released, many leaving the game permanently, and Bradford City, Swindon Town and QPR were just three clubs who went into administration in the wake of the crisis: even today, the collapse of ITV Digital is cited as a key factor in the struggles of many smaller clubs.

FA CUP WINNERS

2000:	Chelsea 1-0 Aston Villa
2001:	Liverpool 2-1 Arsenal
2002:	Arsenal 2-0 Chelsea
2003:	Arsenal 1-0 Southampton
2004:	Manchester United 3-0 Millwall
2005:	Arsenal 0-0 (5/4 pens) Manchester United
2006:	Liverpool 3-3 (3/1 pens) West Ham United

2002:
English Football Hall Of Fame

The English Football Hall of Fame was opened in 2002 as part of the National Football Museum at Preston North End's Deepdale ground. A popular idea among fans and former players and managers, it was set up to recognise the achievements of the very best in the game throughout history. Inaugural inductees in the Hall of Fame (decided by a panel of leading figures from the game) included George Best, Eric Cantona, Bobby Charlton, Tom Finney, Paul Gascoigne, Kevin Keegan, Denis Law, Billy Wright, Stanley Matthews and Bobby Moore, among others, with the managerial list containing the six greatest managers in English football history: Ramsey, Shankly, Paisley, Busby, Clough and Ferguson. A women's category also honours the best female players.

Since 2002, the likes of Tommy Lawton, Geoff Hurst, Jackie Milburn, Alan Shearer, Roy Keane, John Barnes, Alan Hansen and Arsène Wenger have joined the list, alongside Arthur Wharton (England's first black professional, who played for Preston and Sheffield United in the 1880s and 1890s but whose existence was largely unknown until the 1990s).

Left and below: Russian billionaire Roman Abramovich, whose purchase of Chelsea from Ken Bates in 2003 sent shockwaves throughout the footballing world.

2003:
Roman Abramovich Buys Chelsea

For the tabloids, it was the football story of the decade: a mysterious Russian billionaire buys one of Britain's most famous clubs and promises to buy the best players in the world, with money no object. For Chelsea fans, it was a dream come true. But the true implications of Roman Abramovich's involvement with the Stamford Bridge outfit may not be known for many years.

Abramovich's fortune is currently estimated at more than £18 billion, making him one of the world's richest men: his money comes from oil trading in remote Russian provinces, although his background and business dealings are shrouded in secrecy. He paid £60 million to take Chelsea off owner Ken Bates' hands, and immediately spent £100 million on players including Arjen Robben, Adrian Mutu, Hernan Crespo, Claude Makelele and Joe Cole. Chelsea finished the season in second place in the Premiership, but it was not enough to keep Italian coach Claudio Ranieri in a job and he was replaced in 2004 by Jose Mourinho. Abramovich's investment has now passed the £500 million mark, but with such deep pockets he seems content to continue pouring money into the club (and making considerable losses in the process). His arrival at Chelsea has sent transfer inflation into overdrive, and many worry about a general collapse in the European transfer market should he ever leave the club.

2004:
Arsenal Unbeaten

The Manchester United-Arsenal rivalry had seen the league title shared by the pair since 1996; in 2003/04, however, there was to be little competition. Arsène Wenger's team clicked into top gear spectacularly, to wrestle United's championship away from them, becoming only the second team since Preston North End in 1888/89 to go an entire season unbeaten in the process. Wenger had brought in German goalkeeper Jens Lehmann to back up a defence which included Lauren, Sol Campbell, Ashley Cole, Kolo Toure and, occasionally, the veteran Martin Keown.

With Thierry Henry in scintillating form (scoring 30 times in 37 matches) and Robert Pires, Freddie Ljungberg and Dennis Bergkamp supplying the ammunition, nobody could come close to the Gunners, who amassed 90 points to win the title by a clear 11 points. Arsenal had begun an unbeaten run with a 6-1 thrashing of Southampton in May 2003, and it took in the entire 2003/04 season. In the first home match of 2004/05, against Blackburn, Arsenal won 3-0 to record their 43rd consecutive unbeaten game, a new English record. They remained unbeaten until losing a bad-tempered clash with Manchester United at Old Trafford 2-0 in October. Their run had at this point stretched to an incredible 49 matches.

Arsenal players worship the Premiership cup after clinching the title with a 2-2 draw against Tottenham Hotspur in 2004.

Arsenal's impressive new Emirates stadium, after a move from their legendary Highbury home.

2006:
New Arsenal Stadium

Arsenal needed a spectacular new home to replace Highbury, one of the most famous grounds in the game, whose last match had been a 4-2 defeat of Wigan Athletic in May 2006, marked by a Thierry Henry hat-trick. They got it with Ashburton Grove (officially named the Emirates Stadium), within walking distance of the old ground and at 60,200 the second-largest ground in the Premiership behind Old Trafford. The stadium opened in August 2006, but the first scorer there was not an Arsenal player: Aston Villa's Olof Mellberg headed home before Gilberto Silva equalised. Arsenal are the biggest English club to move home in the post-war era, but they will not be the last: Liverpool announced plans in 2006 to relocate to a new 60,000-seater stadium in the city's Stanley Park, possibly in time for 2008/09.

Ashley Cole (b. 1980)

(Arsenal, Chelsea, England)

Previously known simply as a prodigiously talented left-back with a penchant for charging upfield, during 2005 and 2006 Ashley Cole's name was rarely off the back pages thanks to a protracted transfer wrangle involving big-spending Chelsea. The Blues had bought in players from many of the continent's leading clubs but had never moved for one of their fellow title contenders' stars. In the summer of 2005, however, rumour surfaced that Arsenal's Cole had met with Jose Mourinho and Chelsea chief executive Peter Kenyon. Cole was fined £100,000 for having dinner with

Joe Cole made his mark in the 2006 World Cup.

Ashley Cole courted controversy in his move to Chelsea.

the pair in what was widely seen as a case of 'tapping up' (trying to induce a contracted player to switch clubs), and he later claimed Arsenal had 'fed him to the sharks' by not defending him properly. He finally joined Chelsea in summer 2006, for £5 million plus William Gallas.

Joe Cole (b. 1981)

(West Ham, Chelsea, England)

Joe Cole followed international team-mate Frank Lampard from West Ham to Chelsea in 2003, to become another member of the all-star cast at Stamford Bridge. Cole had made his first West Ham appearance at

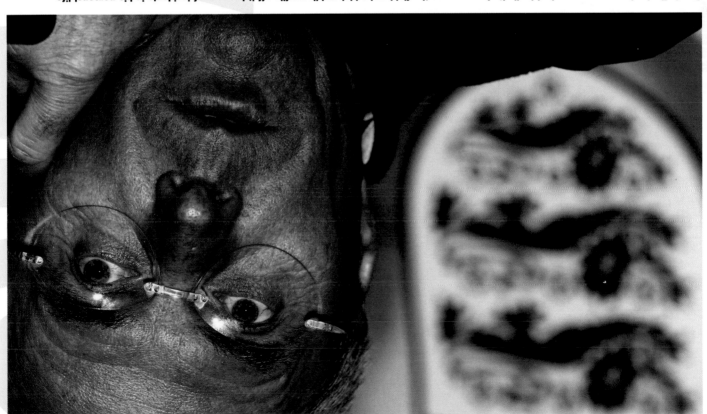

Sven's England career was marked by limited success on the field and a high public profile off it because of incidents in his personal life.

16, but had been hyped as the best young talent in the game for two years before that thanks to a series of fervent tabloid reports about his talent. As a professional, Cole's dribbling and array of skills make him one of the most naturally talented English players of his generation, but he still found it hard to hold down a starting place on Chelsea's wings for some time. In 2005/06 he began playing more regularly and finished the season as one of England's best players at the 2006 World Cup, scoring a sublime goal against Sweden.

Sven-Göran Eriksson (b. 1948)

(P: Torsby (Sweden), Karlskoga (Sweden); M: IFK Gothenburg, Benfica, Roma, Fiorentina, Sampdoria, Lazio, England)

In 2001, Swede Sven-Göran Eriksson became England's first-ever foreign coach, dividing opinion across the nation. His performance over the next five years did little to change the minds of those who claimed the national team should have looked closer to home. Eriksson had enjoyed considerable success in Italy, and at first he seemed an inspired choice for England, leading the team to an historic 5-1 World Cup qualifying win in Germany in September 2001. His record in qualifiers was excellent, but after poor displays in the 2002 World Cup and 2004 European Championship finals, questions were asked about his tactical abilities. High-profile affairs with TV presenter Ulrika Jonsson and FA secretary Faria Alam did not help his case; nor did an interview with a tabloid newspaper journalist posing as a sheikh, in which Eriksson claimed he would walk away from England to join Aston Villa. In January 2006, it was announced he would leave his job after that summer's World Cup.

FOOTBALL WRITERS' ASSOCIATION FOOTBALLER OF THE YEAR

2000:	Roy Keane	Manchester United
2001:	Teddy Sheringham	Manchester United
2002:	Robert Pires	Arsenal
2003:	Thierry Henry	Arsenal
2004:	Thierry Henry	Arsenal
2005:	Frank Lampard	Chelsea
2006:	Thierry Henry	Arsenal

Thierry Henry is known for his flair on and off the pitch.

Rio Ferdinand (b. 1978)

(West Ham, Leeds United, Manchester United, England)

The massive transfer fees paid for Rio Ferdinand are testimony to his position as one of England's most forward-thinking defenders ever. The London-born centre-half loves to get forward, in the style of an Italian libero rather than a traditional, rugged English enforcer. Ferdinand cost Leeds £18 million when he left his first club, West Ham, in 2000; when he crossed the Pennines for Manchester United two years later, the fee was £30 million. Ferdinand has also established himself as an England regular and starred in the 1998, 2002 and 2006 World Cups, but he courted controversy in 2003 when he failed to attend a drugs test; though he passed a re-test, he was banned from the game for eight months.

The highly priced Rio Ferdinand.

Steven Gerrard (b. 1980)

(Liverpool, England)

Despite his tender years, Steven Gerrard is already on course to become Liverpool's most popular player ever. His dynamic midfield performances, superb attitude and well-timed runs into the box have made him the first name on the Reds' team sheet, and the team has effectively been built around him for several years. Lifelong fan Gerrard made his Liverpool bow in November 1997, first appeared for England in 2000, and

Frank Lampard (b. 1978)

(West Ham, Chelsea, England)

T he son of former West Ham player and assistant boss Frank Lampard senior stepped out of his father's shadow to become 'the best player in the world' according to his Chelsea manager, Jose Mourinho. Lampard had joined the Blues for £11 million in 2001, and soon justified the fee with his all-action displays in the team's engine room. In 2004/05, he played in every match as Chelsea won the title. He made his international debut in 1999, but has often been criticised as his England performances are perceived to be less dynamic than those for Chelsea; many believe he and fellow midfielder Steven Gerrard are too similar to play in the same team.

Frank Lampard has been criticised for his England performances.

was made club captain in 2002. He was widely linked with Chelsea in 2004/05 but publicly decided to stick with his first love in the summer of 2005, following his finest hour in the shirt during the thrilling Champions League final.

Thierry Henry (b. 1977)

(Monaco, Juventus, Arsenal, France)

I n October 2005, Thierry Henry's two goals for Arsenal against Sparta Prague meant he became the club's top goalscorer of all time, with 186 to his name in all competitions – and all before the age of 28. Henry had become arguably the Premiership's most accomplished player, with his searing pace matched only by his finishing and his delight in showing his full range of exuberant skills (including an audacious back-heeled goal against Charlton in 2004). He started his career under Arsène Wenger at Monaco, before enduring a torrid time as a winger with Juventus, playing just 13 times. Wenger took him to Highbury, moved him up front, and he has delighted his own and opposing supporters ever since, rejecting advances from Real Madrid and Barcelona, among others.

Ever-popular England and Liverpool midfielder Steven Gerrard.

Jose Mourinho (b. 1963)
(M: Benfica, Leiria (Portugal), Porto, Chelsea)

Nobody could accuse Jose Mourinho of being short on confidence. Though his playing career never got above amateur level, as a manager the Portuguese showman is the self-proclaimed 'Special One' and architect of Chelsea's first title triumph for 50 years. He joined the London club in 2004 after a remarkable career in his native land, and immediately instilled a new sense of belief and vigour in the team, as well as spending owner Roman Abramovich's millions on some of the world's best players and getting them into a brilliant unit which proved almost unbeatable. Mourinho is not scared of courting controversy, frequently criticising referees, the Football Association and, in particular, Arsenal and their boss Arsene Wenger, who he famously labelled a 'voyeur' who loved talking about Chelsea rather than his own club.

Chelsea manager Jose Mourinho.

Michael Owen (b. 1979)
(Liverpool, Real Madrid, Newcastle, England)

Michael Owen burst onto the football scene at the 1998 World Cup, when he won himself a regular starting place in the England team and scored a wonderful goal against Argentina to earn the attention of Pele, Diego Maradona and others. Chester-born Owen had just completed his first full season with Liverpool and would go on to score 118 goals in 216 appearances for them. He surprised many by joining Real Madrid for £8 million in 2004 and struggled to get into the Spanish giants' starting XI. Come August 2005, he was being linked with a return to England (and possibly to either Liverpool or Manchester United), but only Newcastle could meet Real's valuation and Owen enjoyed an injury-hit first season which got even worse with a broken metatarsal bone at the 2006 World Cup keeping him out until mid-2007 at the earliest.

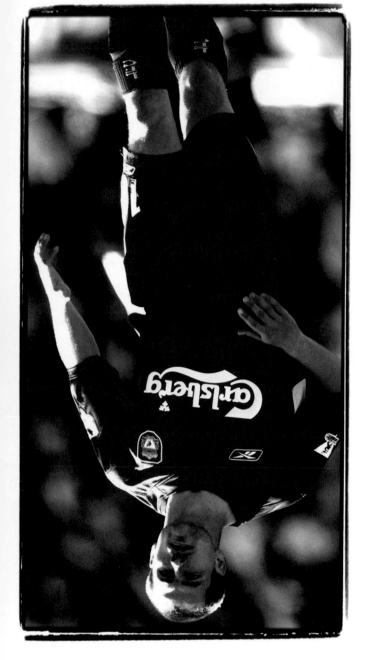

Michael Owen has failed to live up to early promise because of injury.

Robert Pires (b. 1973)

(Metz, Marseille, Arsenal, Villareal, France)

A World Cup and European Championship winner, winger Robert Pires joined Arsenal in 2000 and immediately struck up a rapport with countryman Thierry Henry which was to be a major factor in Arsenal's 2002 and 2004 title victories. Frequently laying on the passes for Henry's goals, Pires overcame some initial indifferent form to draw widespread acclaim for his all-round ability. He left London in 2006 to sign for Spanish side Villareal.

Wayne Rooney (b. 1985)

(Everton, Manchester United, England)

B oy wonder and occasional hothead, Wayne Rooney is the most exciting English talent of his generation – a powerful forward as adept at setting up others with intelligent play as scoring spectacular goals himself. He found the net for Everton five days before his 17th birthday to become the youngest Premiership scorer at the time, but after a sensational performance in England's doomed 2004 European Championship campaign which made him the talk of the continent, he joined Manchester United for £31 million. Rooney has a reputation for being short-tempered which has occasionally overshadowed his undoubted natural talent: after winning the race to get fit enough for the 2006 World Cup finals, he was sent off in England's quarter-final with Portugal.

Boy wonder Wayne Rooney – widely considered the most exciting player of his generation.

John Terry took the baton as England captain when David Beckham stepped down after World Cup 2006.

John Terry (b. 1980)

(Chelsea, England)

John Terry's no-nonsense displays for Chelsea and England have seen him shackle some of the world's best players. Not much gets past the powerful central defender, who is as strong in the air as he is in the tackle and has reigned in the wilder side of his temperament to become a model professional for club and country. He came through the Chelsea ranks and first appeared for the first team in 1998. He was made captain by Jose Mourinho and lifted the Premiership trophy in 2005, having already starred for England in Euro 2004. Terry became England captain when David Beckham stepped down from the role in 2006.

Ruud van Nistelrooy (b. 1976)

(Den Bosch (Holland), Heerenveen (Holland), PSV Eindhoven, Manchester United, Real Madrid, Netherlands)

Deadly Dutch striker Ruud van Nistelrooy joined Manchester United in 2001 after being identified by Sir Alex Ferguson as the goalscorer he needed to add the finishing touches to his side. The Dutchman hit 23 during his first season, which included scoring in eight consecutive games; he scored 25 the following season as United won the title. Van Nistelrooy continued to find the net with amazing regularity over the next three years, but late in the 2005/06 season began to be dropped from the team amid talk of a behind-the-scenes rift.

Theo Walcott (b. 1989)

(Southampton, Arsenal, England)

Talented teenage players find themselves under huge media scrutiny, but England's newest sensation, Theo Walcott, has equipped himself well in his fledgling career. The pacy young forward was being touted as a future international as soon as he broke into the Southampton first team; his excellent form for a struggling side saw him picked up by Arsenal for an initial £5 million in early 2006. Although Arsène Wenger kept Walcott out of the first team, citing the need to protect him to aid his development, amazingly this did not stop Sven-Göran Eriksson selecting him for that summer's World Cup squad. Despite being short on strikers after injuries to Wayne Rooney and Michael Owen, Eriksson resisted the temptation to play Walcott in the finals themselves.

Dutch import Ruud van Nistelrooy.

He left for Real Madrid in July 2006 and has since continued to score regularly for his new club.

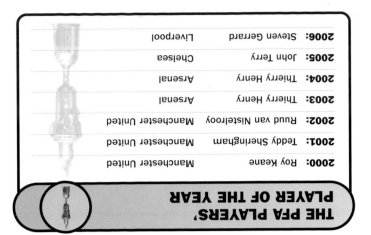

Touted as the next big thing – Theo Walcott.

THE PFA PLAYERS' PLAYER OF THE YEAR

2000:	Roy Keane	Manchester United
2001:	Teddy Sheringham	Manchester United
2002:	Ruud van Nistelrooy	Manchester United
2003:	Thierry Henry	Arsenal
2004:	Thierry Henry	Arsenal
2005:	John Terry	Chelsea
2006:	Steven Gerrard	Liverpool

Michael Owen hits the deck in the UEFA Cup final between Liverpool and Alaves, May 2001.

MATCHES

Liverpool 5-4 Alaves
UEFA Cup Final, Dortmund, 16 May 2001

Liverpool: (Man. Gerard Houllier) Westerveld, Henchoz (Smicer), Hyypia, Babbel, Carragher, Gerrard, Murphy, Hamann, McAllister, Owen (Berger), Heskey (Fowler)

Alaves: (Man. José Manuel Esnal) Herrera, Geli, Contra, Eggen (Alonso), Karmona, Tellez, Desio, Astudillo (Magno), Tomic, Moreno (Pablo), Cruyff

Scorers: Liverpool: Babbel 4, Gerard 16, McAllister 41 (pen), Fowler 73, Geli 117 og; Alaves: Alonso 27, Moreno 48, 51, Cruyff 89

Liverpool landed their first post-Heysel European trophy the hard way, with an extra-time own goal from Delfi Geli giving them victory under the Golden Goal rule. The match was a personal triumph for veteran midfielder Gary McAllister, a surprising signing the previous summer who ran the show and whipped in the corner which later led to the Reds' winner. Liverpool were 3-1 up at half-time, but a last-minute strike from former Manchester United winger Jordi Cruyff sent the game into extra time and the Spanish minnows, in their first European competition, had two men sent off before capitulating.

Germany 1-5 England
World Cup Qualifier, Munich, 1 September 2001

Germany: (Man. Rudi Völler) Kahn, Worns (Asamoah), Rehmer, Linke, Nowotny, Bohme, Hamann, Ballack (Klose), Deisler, Jancker, Neuville (Kehl)

England: (Man. Sven Göran Eriksson) Seaman, G. Neville, Cole, Campbell, Ferdinand, Gerrard (Hargreaves), Scholes (Carragher), Beckham, Barmby (McManaman), Heskey, Owen

Scorers: Germany: Jancker; England: Owen 13, 48, 66, Gerrard 45, Heskey 74

Tottenham Hotspur 3-5 Manchester United

Premiership, White Hart Lane, 29 September 2001

Tottenham: (Man. Glenn Hoddle) Sullivan, Taricco, King, Perry, Richards, Ziege, Freund, Anderton (Rebrov), Poyet, Ferdinand, Sheringham

Manchester United: (Man. Alex Ferguson) Barthez, G. Neville, Blanc, Johnsen, Irwin (Silvestre), Beckham, Butt (Solskjaer), Scholes, Veron, Cole, van Nistelrooy

Scorers: Tottenham: Richards 15, Ferdinand 25, Ziege 45; Manchester United: Cole 46, Blanc 58, van Nistelrooy 72, Veron 76, Beckham 87

The most dramatic comeback the Premiership has ever seen, and a fascinating game of football for neutrals. Coming back from three-down away from home is a huge test of character, but having gone in seemingly dead and buried for the break at White Hart Lane, Manchester United re-emerged to play 45 minutes of blistering football.

Andy Cole netted within a minute of the restart and Sir Alex Ferguson's men were level by 72 minutes. Juan Veron and David Beckham both found the net to put the result beyond doubt and leave Spurs in shock.

FOOTBALL LEAGUE CHAMPIONS

2000/01:	Manchester United
2001/02:	Arsenal
2002/03:	Manchester United
2003/04:	Arsenal
2004/05:	Chelsea
2005/06:	Chelsea

Given the troubled history between these two sides, stretching back to 1966, a World Cup qualifying trip to Munich was not a match England were relishing. But under new coach Sven-Göran Eriksson, self-belief kicked in and everything the visitors tried came right on a remarkable evening in Munich. Carsten Jancker put Germany ahead, but it was the only thing that went right for them all night; Michael Owen ran rings around the defence and ended up with a hat-trick, while Germany had no answer to Emile Heskey's power. The photo of the stadium's electronic scoreboard showing England 5-1 ahead is one of the most powerful images in English football history, behind only Bobby Moore lifting the World Cup and Paul Gascoigne's tears in 1990.

Below: Sheringham tries to stop the landslide.

Above: Michael Owen's finest hour – a hat-trick against Germany.

Liverpool 3-3 AC Milan
Champions League Final, Istanbul, 25 May 2005

Liverpool: (Man. Gerard Houllier) Dudek, Finnan (Hamann), Traore, Hyypia, Carragher, Riise, Gerrard, Garcia, Alonso, Kewell (Smicer), Baros (Cisse).

Milan: (Man. Rafael Benitez) Dida, Cafu, Maldini, Stam, Nesta, Gattuso (Rui Costa), Seedorf (Serginho), Pirlo, Kaka, Shevchenko, Crespo (Tomasson).

Scorers: Liverpool: Gerrard 54, Smicer 56, Alonso 59; Milan: Maldini 1, Crespo 39, 44.

A classic final and an incredible comeback made Liverpool's 2005 Champions League win the most dramatic and satisfying English triumph in Europe of all time. Three-down at half-time, Liverpool's fairytale run to the final seemed certain to be over. Many fans watching at home simply switched off the television – and they missed a classic. Star-studded Milan had gone ahead inside a minute thanks to legendary captain Paolo Maldini, and two further first-half goals from Hernan Crespo seemed to have put the result beyond doubt as the Italians dominated.

Argentina 0-1 England
World Cup First Round, Sapporo, 7 June 2002

Argentina: (Man. Marcelo Bielsa) Cavallero, Sorin, Samuel, Pochettino, Placente, Zanetti, Simeone, Veron (Aimar), Gonzalez (Lopez), Ortega, Batistuta (Crespo).

England: (Man. Sven-Goran Eriksson) Seaman, Mills, Cole, Hargreaves (Sinclair), Ferdinand, Campbell, Beckham, Scholes, Butt, Owen (Bridge), Heskey (Sheringham).

Scorer: England: Beckham 44 (pen)

David Beckham achieved redemption for his 1998 dismissal in the most effective way imaginable, when his spot-kick before half-time gave England victory over Argentina and paved the way for passage into the second round of the 2002 World Cup. Beckham stepped up after Michael Owen had tumbled (some might say a little too easily) over Mauricio Pochettino. England dug deep for a memorable victory, but after trouncing Denmark they met favourites Brazil in the heat of Shizuoka and Michael Owen's goal was not enough to prevent a 2-1 defeat sealed by Ronaldinho's long-range free-kick over David Seaman.

Diego Placente and David Beckham battle it out in the 2002 World Cup first round, England v. Argentina.

Wayne Rooney is shown the red card for stamping on Portugal's Ricardo Carvalho.

Portugal: (Man. Luiz Felipe Scolari) Ricardo, Miguel, Meira, Carvalho, Valente, Figo (Postiga), Maniche, Petit, Tiago (Viana), Ronaldo, Pauleta (Simao)

England: (Man. Sven-Goran Eriksson) Robinson, G. Neville, Terry, Ferdinand, A. Cole, Hargreaves, Beckham (Lennon (Carragher)), Gerrard, Lampard, J. Cole (Crouch), Rooney

England 0-0
Portugal
World Cup Quarter
Final, Gelsenkirchen,
1 July 2006

England's World Cup finals journey under Sven-Göran Eriksson (who had announced he would leave after the tournament) had been a mixed bag by the time they played an equally disappointing Portugal in the quarter-finals. Injury had ruled out Michael Owen in the group stages, and with Wayne Rooney only just back from a serious injury, England were desperately short of fit, experienced strikers. They had laboured to see off minnows Paraguay and Trinidad and Tobago in the group stages, leading to furious headlines back home, and had also made hard work of surprise packages Ecuador in the second round.

Against Portugal, the performance was much improved but the outcome all too familiar. In a scrappy game, neither side could stamp their authority but England looked the more settled and showed some of the passion the public had been demanding before the match. In Rooney's case, however, it boiled over in the 62nd minute, when he appeared to stamp on Ricardo Carvalho in what the England striker later claimed was simply an unfortunate tangle. As players joined in the melee, Rooney pushed Manchester United team-mate Cristiano Ronaldo, who had earlier appeared to wind him up as the teams waited for kick-off. Rooney got the red card, Ronaldo was caught winking at the Portuguese bench and became a hate figure in England – and Eriksson's men had to hold on for an hour to earn another penalty shoot-out. England capitulated again, scoring just once as Portugal won 3-1 from the spot.

keep the trophy outright.

Chelsea as emotion poured out all over the stadium. The win was Liverpool's fifth European Cup and meant they could

Steven Gerrard lifts the UEFA Champions League trophy.

But Liverpool came out for the second period a changed team, and they were level before the hour as Steven Gerrard's header, Vladimir Smicer's long-ranger and Xavi Alonso's follow-up from a saved penalty left Milan stunned. It was the English side who looked the more likely to win the match, but extra-time and then penalties beckoned to complete an emotional rollercoaster of an evening. Jerzy Dudek imitated former Liverpool goalkeeper Bruce Grobbelaar as he tried to put off kick-takers with eccentric behaviour on the line. Liverpool led 3-2 as Andriy Shevchenko stepped up to take Milan's fifth penalty. Polish keeper Dudek saved, and Liverpool were victorious. A delighted Gerrard lifted the trophy and was soon scotching rumours he would join

TEAMS

Arsenal 1998–2004

Arsène Wenger

Key Players: Thierry Henry (striker), Jens Lehmann (goalkeeper), Patrick Vieira (midfielder)

Trophies: Premiership 1998, 2002, 2004; FA Cup 1998, 2002, 2003

When Arsène Wenger arrived at Highbury in 1996 to become Arsenal's first-ever foreign manager, he inherited a club which had lost its way dramatically since the glory days of George Graham.

Complete Overhaul

Arsenal had finished fifth the previous season and looked no match for Alex Ferguson's slick Manchester United team; many of their players were past their best and there were no obvious replacements waiting in the wings. Wenger started from scratch and was so successful so quickly that in the summer of 1998 a national newspaper claimed Arsenal had 'won the World Cup' for their contribution of two key players as France lifted football's ultimate prize.

New Blood

Wenger was an advocate of sports science and immediately overhauled training methods, diet and rehabilitation from injury, as well as introducing a

worldwide scouting network which would bring the best young players from every corner of the globe to north London. More immediately, he brought in a number of key players who had been overlooked by their present clubs and were hungry to succeed (some of them were French, but all of them were foreign – in February 2005,

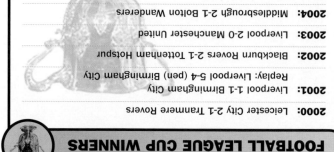

FOOTBALL LEAGUE CUP WINNERS

2000:	Leicester City 2-1 Tranmere Rovers
2001:	Liverpool 1-1 Birmingham City Replay: Liverpool 5-4 (pen) Birmingham City
2002:	Blackburn Rovers 2-1 Tottenham Hotspur
2003:	Liverpool 2-0 Manchester United
2004:	Middlesbrough 2-1 Bolton Wanderers
2005:	Chelsea 3-2 Liverpool
2006:	Manchester United 4-0 Wigan Athletic

241

Arsène Wenger's superlative 2003 FA Cup-winning team.

HISTORY OF ENGLISH FOOTBALL · 2000 AND BEYOND

not one member of the Arsenal playing squad for a match against Crystal Palace was English).

A Great Rivalry

Wenger's first cash signing was arguably his most important, as he plucked Patrick Vieira from Milan's reserves and made the snarling, no-nonsense ball-winner the key figure in the Arsenal midfield. Vieira, like the side as a whole, would be criticised for the number of cards he collected with his physical style, but never his commitment to the cause. He was partnered by Emmanuel Petit as Arsenal finished third in Wenger's first season and won the double in 1998, thanks

to the goals of Ian Wright and Dennis Bergkamp. Thierry Henry came in to replace Wright, but Arsenal finished runners-up to Manchester United in each of the next three seasons, developing a fierce rivalry with the Old Trafford club which was most clearly manifested in animosity between Wenger and Ferguson. Arsenal gained a spectacular revenge in 2004, as they won the league at Old Trafford after going the whole season unbeaten, part of a 49-game run without defeat. The Gunners' next challenge is to re-establish themselves after Chelsea upped the Premiership ante with their free-spending antics. If Wenger stays at the helm, do not bet against them......

Chelsea 2003–?
Jose Mourinho

Key Players: Petr Cech (goalkeeper), John Terry (defender), Frank Lampard (midfielder)

Trophies: Premiership 2005, 2006; League Cup 2005

Roman Abramovich's sensational purchase of Chelsea in 2003 may have dismayed purists and led to huge inflation in the transfer market, but at Stamford Bridge it has been one long party for delirious Chelsea fans.

A Long Time Coming

The club had been starved of success for years: in the early part of the twentieth century, their failure to win any trophies was a running joke, and though they finally landed the championship in 1955 they were better known in the 1960s and 1970s for being a 'glamour club' with film-star supporters and in the 1980s for their hooligan element. Abramovich changed all that, but it cost him hundreds of millions to do so. In his first season in charge alone, he presided over £100 million of purchases made by Italian manager Claudio Ranieri, including Damien Duff (£17 million), Hernan Crespo (£16.8 million) and Claude Makelele (£16.6 million). Yet Ranieri, likeable as he was, could only finish second in the Premiership when Abramovich and the fans expected nothing less than the title, and he paid with his job.

A Dream Season

The Russian brought in Jose Mourinho, one of the most highly rated young managers in Europe, who exuded confidence and swagger. It rubbed off on the team immediately, and with new £24 million striker Didier Drogba providing an extra cutting edge, Chelsea were pacesetters all season. John Terry and Frank Lampard had come of age at the heart of the team and Petr Cech had established himself as the finest goalkeeper in the world. Nobody could stop the Londoners: they beat Manchester United 1–0 in their first match of the season and never looked back as they took the title in their centenary year, 50 years after their first title victory. Only defeat to Liverpool over two dramatic matches in the semi-finals of the Champions League spoiled the season – the quest for European domination would take longer.

A Blank Cheque

Mourinho added a few reinforcements just for good measure in summer 2005: £24 million Michael Essien and £21 million England international Shaun Wright-Phillips. The Blues won the league by eight points. With Abramovich's fortune barely even dented by his huge spending to date, the question for the rest of the Premiership is: will he one day get bored or is every other major club destined to play second fiddle to Chelsea's Russian revolution?

AMPIONS

2004 ~ 2005

Chelsea team members lap up the attention after winning the Premiership.

AFC Wimbledon (2002–?) and FC United (2005–?)

Trophies: English: Combined Counties League 2004, Ryman League Division One 2005 (AFC Wimbledon); North West Counties League Division One 2006 (FC United)

Supporter-owned clubs were not a new phenomenon in English football: as a number of clubs had experienced severe financial difficulties in the late 1990s, fans had got together to buy some outright (Exeter, Bournemouth) and had made significant investments in others. But the rise of AFC Wimbledon and FC United has been something else altogether: driven not by financial necessity but by indignation at the behaviour of those in power and the belief that fan-ownership is the only way to ensure clubs are run properly and fairly.

AFC Wimbledon

AFC Wimbledon came into being when former FA Cup winners Wimbledon (who had been relegated and were ground-sharing with Crystal Palace) were given permission by the FA to relocate to Milton Keynes, more than 112 km (70 miles) away from their south London fanbase, where they claimed they could not find a suitable ground of their own and did not have enough supporters to be financially viable. Outraged Dons fans immediately set up their own

club and began playing at a low rung of non-league football, taking more than 2,000 supporters to tiny grounds in the Combined Counties League and attracting 3,000-plus at home as they attempted to climb back up the pyramid. They made it to the Ryman League in 2004, while Milton Keynes Dons (as they were now known) dropped to League Two and failed to attract more supporters than the old Wimbledon had. Wimbledon's heritage and history was officially handed to AFC in 2006.

FC United

For FC United of Manchester, the catalyst was the takeover of Manchester United in 2005 by US tycoon Malcolm Glazer and his family. For supporters who had already fought a Rupert Murdoch takeover, it was a step too far and they feared life at the top of the Premiership had become solely about money rather than passion; a breakaway group formed a new club called FC United and revelled in the simple pleasures of the non-league game, winning the North West Counties League Division One title at the first time of asking as more than 3,000 fans regularly turned out at Bury's Gigg Lane ground. AFC Wimbledon and FC United's respective rises are unlikely to be the end of supporter-owned clubs: the real test, however, will be whether a professional team can one day rely on its supporters alone.

Fan-owned clubs might be the future of football in England.

FEATURES

The Millionaire Footballer

I n 2006, David Beckham topped the Football Rich List with a total value of £75 million. Ten British players in all were reckoned to be worth £20 million or more each, but that figure is dwarfed on the continent, where Ronaldinho was believed to be taking home £15 million a year in 2006.

The Bosman Ruling

How had footballers gone from the days of the maximum wage being abolished in the early 1960s, when £100 per week was reckoned to be an extravagant wage, to earnings which put captains of industry and Hollywood actors to shame? The change can be traced back to the Bosman ruling in 1995, when a Belgian second division player called Jean-Marc Bosman was refused a move to a French team by his existing club, even though his contract had expired. He took his case to the European Court of Justice in Luxembourg, arguing that as he was out of contract he was a free agent and his club could not demand a transfer fee for his services. He won, and football was left with no choice but to abolish the retain-and-transfer system; although agreed safeguards were built in to ensure clubs were

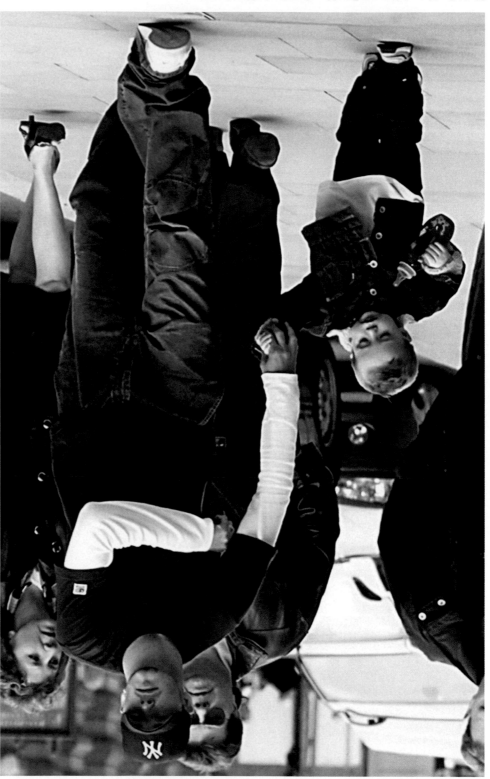

David Beckham takes son Brooklyn shopping in Manchester.

compensated when players under the age of 23 left them, others could move freely when their contracts ended.

The Rich Get Richer

The Bosman ruling was bad news for small clubs, who were less sure of a future transfer income, and for lower league players, who faced increased uncertainty about their futures; but it was a massive boost for leading players, who could now auction their services when their contracts ended and join the club paying the highest wages rather than the one their current employers agreed a transfer fee with. This increased power led to huge rises in players' wages during the late 1990s.

Ashley Cole with partner and pop star Cheryl Tweedy.

And as they got richer, players' agents got cannier, insisting on image-rights payments from clubs which meant players received money when clubs marketed their likeness or skills (such as selling T-shirts or DVDs linked to a particular player). Sportswear contracts, too, grew ever more lucrative as players' individual profiles were raised through increased media exposure; Thierry Henry picked up £9 million to endorse Reebok boots, while less than a third of Beckham's total income in 2006 was thought to be his Real Madrid wages, as he was involved with numerous sponsorships and endorsement deals.

Steven Gerrard's girlfriend Alex Curran enjoys the sights of Baden Baden during the Germany 2006 World Cup.

Foreign Players vs Homegrown Talent

While headlines today lament the foreign 'invasion' of the Premiership, which has elevated English football to the number one destination for talent from around the globe, foreigners first plied their trade in the English game a century ago.

Few And Far Between

German Max Seeburg appeared for Tottenham during their first season in the league, in 1907, and later played for Chelsea and Burnley before being imprisoned during the First World War for having the wrong papers. Yet although there were notable exceptions – including Manchester City's famous German goalkeeper Bert Trautmann, West Ham's Bermudan striker Clyde Best and Leeds' South African Albert Johanneson, one of the first prominent black players in the top flight – foreigners were few and far between for most of the twentieth century.

Flair And Finesse

When Spurs' Argentinian duo Ricky Villa and Ossie Ardiles made such an impact at White Hart Lane in the late 1970s, clubs began to see the value of imported talent, to add flair and finesse which could sometimes be in short supply among British players. In the 1990s, as wages and transfer budgets rose dramatically with the advent of the Premiership, an ever-increasing number of foreigners came to England: the likes of Eric Cantona, Gianfranco Zola and Jurgen Klinsmann were among the best in the world at the time and their presence helped persuade other top talents to consider England as a real alternative to Spain or Italy.

Here To Stay

Smaller clubs were soon also importing foreigners – not just dazzling showmen but also more everyday defenders or midfielders from Scandinavia or Eastern Europe, who could be signed more cheaply than an emerging player from a lower league club in England. There were 37 foreigners in the first season of the Premiership, a figure which reached the 200 mark in the year 2000 and was approaching 250 in 2006. Only two clubs in the entire Football League had no players from outside the UK at the last count, and in the 2006/07 season only four out of 20

Left: Sardinian Gianfranco Zola. Above: Frenchman Eric Cantona.

Premiership clubs had first-choice English goalkeepers (with only six from the UK as a whole). On Boxing Day 1999, Chelsea became the first club to field a starting XI in the Premiership without a single Englishman.

Investing In The Future?

While it is undoubtedly true that the skills foreign players have brought to the Premiership have helped make for more entertaining matches and a better spectacle for fans (and supporters of Arsenal and Chelsea embrace their foreign stars every bit as readily as their English players), the number of foreigners has a detrimental effect on the England team; what is particularly worrying is the way big clubs, particularly Arsenal, Chelsea and Manchester United, have begun importing promising teenagers to join their youth teams, preventing English youngsters from even experiencing top coaching in the first place, let alone making the first team. When even English internationals are being left out of the squad at Chelsea to make way for an array of foreign talent, it is not xenophobic to worry about the future of the international team.

GLOSSARY

Advantage: Referee can waive foul if fouled team will benefit.

Assistant Referee: Formerly known as linesman.

Blind-side: Position on opposite side of an opponent to the ball.

By-line: The goal-line.

Cambridge Rules: The game's first set of rules drawn up in 1848.

Campynge: Early Suffolk name for game similar to football.

Cautions: Punishment given to player for serious or persistent foul play.

Centre-back: Centrally positioned defence.

Chip: Quickly lifting the ball into the air.

Corner-kick: Awarded to attacking team when ball kicked over by-line by defender.

Cross: Ball played to a team-mate from a wide position.

Cut back: Ball played back from goal-line at sharp angle.

Direct free-kick: Awarded for serious infringement of the rules.

Dribble: Attacker taking the ball past a defender.

Dummy: Feinting to move in one direction and going the other to trick a defender.

'Engine Room': Nickname given to unit of midfield players.

Extra-time: 30 minutes added when teams are level after normal time.

FA Cup: World's oldest knockout football competition.

FA Premiership: League introduced in 1992 involving top 22 clubs in England.

Far Post: Goal post furthest from the ball.

FIFA: International Federation of Association Football. Governing body for the game worldwide.

Football Association, The: Governing body in England.

Football League list: Panel of referees and assistants who officiate professional matches in England.

Forcing play: Pushing opponents in one direction.

Formation: The way a team lines up.

Foul: Breach of the Laws of the Game.

Full-back: Player in wide defending position.

Goal-area: 5.5 m (6 yd) area drawn from goal posts.

Goal hanger: Slang for a forward who rarely runs back to defend.

Goal-kick: Awarded to defending team when ball is kicked over goal-line by attacker.

Golden Goal: Goal which ends a match in extra-time.

Hapasatum: Roman game which provided football's early origins.

Holding role: Player positioned in front of defenders.

Indirect free-kick: Awarded to less serious offences.

Kick-off: Start of a match, or re-start after half-time and after a goal is scored.

Libero: Another name for sweeper.

Man-for-man marking: Marking one opponent exclusively.

Mark: Follow an opponent to prevent them receiving the ball.

Midfielder: Player in central position.

Near Post: Goal post nearest to the ball.

Obstruction: Blocking an opponent's path.

Offside: A player is in an offside position if he is nearer to his opponents' goal-line than both the ball and the second last opponent.

Overlap: Run outside and beyond a team-mate.

Pass: Propelling ball to team-mate.

Pass and move: System of play developed by Liverpool FC.

Penalty: Awarded if attacking player is fouled in the penalty area.

Penalty area: 16.5 m (18 yd) area marked around the goal.

Penalty shootout: Sudden death way of deciding drawn matches.

Pre-match: Before a game.

Referee: Person responsible for interpreting play and imposing Laws of the Game.

Rotating: Players interchanging positions on the field.

Screen: Player positioned in front of defence to break up attacks early.

Space: Increasing the distance between opponents.

Squeeze: Pushing opponents back into confined space.

Striker: Forward player; chief responsibility to score goals.

Sweeper: Defending position introduced by Italians in 1960s.

Tackle: Challenge with the feet to win the ball.

Tactics: Methods of play used to beat opponents.

Target man: Striker used to receive long passes from defence.

Throw-in: Awarded when the ball crosses the touchline.

Total football: Playing system invented by Holland in the 1970s.

Touch judges: Forerunners of linesman and assistant referees.

Touchline: Line marking the side of the pitch.

UEFA: Union of European Football Associations.

Up and down: Running from one end of the pitch to the other.

Volley: Kicking the ball before it bounces.

Wall pass: Pass between two players to exclude a defender.

WM Formation: English system used in early twentieth century.

Wing-back: Wide positioned player who defends and attacks.

Zonal defending: System of defence where defenders mark opponents in defined areas of the pitch.

FURTHER INFORMATION

Books

Arthur, M., *The Busby Babes: Men of Magic* (Mainstream, 1998)

Davies, H., *The Glory Game* (Mainstream Sport, 2000)

Davies P., *I Lost my Heart to the Belles* (Carnegie, 1997)

Dunphy, E., *Only a Game?* (Penguin, 1987)

Galvin R., *The National Football Museum's Hall of Fame* (Robson Books, 2005)

Glanville, B., *The Story of the World Cup* (Faber and Faber, 2005)

Hornby, N., *Fever Pitch* (Penguin, 2000)

Hugman, B., *The PFA and Premier League Players' Records 1946–2005* (Queen Anne Press, 2005)

Hutchinson, R., *'66: The Inside Story of England's 1966 World Cup Triumph* (Mainstream, 2002)

Kuper, S., *Football Against the Enemy* (Orion, 2002)

Meek, D., *George Best: Tribute to a Legend* (Weidenfeld & Nicholson, 2005)

Powell, J., *Bobby Moore: The Life and Times of a Sporting Hero* (Robson Books, 2002)

Rollin, J., *Sky Sports Football Yearbook* (Headline, 2006)

Russell, D., *Football and the English* (Carnegie Publishing, 1997)

Ward, A. & Taylor, R. P., *Kicking and Screaming: An Oral History of Football in England* (Robson Books, 1998)

Williams, R., *Football Babylon* (Virgin Books, 1996)

Websites

National Football Museum: www.nationalfootballmuseum.com/

Soccerbase: www.soccerbase.com/

Picture Credits

Bridgeman Art Library: 12-13

British Library: 10, 25 (t)

Corbis: 104 (tr), 105, 106-7

Empics: 28, 38, 42-3, 44-5 (b), 46-7, 50 (l), 50 (r), 51 (l), 51 (r), 52, 53, 54-5, 56, 57 (b), 62 (t), 62-3 (b), 65, 66-7, 68, 69, 70 (t), 70 (b), 71 (t), 71 (b), 72 (l), 72 (r), 73 (t), 73 (b), 75, 76-7, 78-9, 80, 81, 83, 86, 87, 89, 88, 90(l), 91 (l), 91 (r), 92 (l), 92 (r), 93 (l), 93 (r), 94 (b), 94 (r), 95 (t), 95 (b), 96 (t), 96 (b), 97 (tl), 97 (tr), 97 (b), 98 (t), 99 (t), 100-1, 102-3, 107 (br), 110, 111, 112, 113, 114, 115 (bl), 115 (tr), 116 (l), 116 (r), 117 (t), 117 (b), 118 (tl), 118 (b), 118 (t), 119, 120, 121 (tl), 121 (bl), 121 (br), 122, 123 (tl), 123 (br), 127, 128, 129, 130-1, 132-3, 134 (b), 135 (t), 135 (b), 136 (b), 137 (t), 137 (b), 140, 141, 142 (l), 143 (r), 143 (l), 144 (l), 144 (bl), 145 (r), 146 (l), 146 (r), 147 (l), 147 (r), 148 (l), 148 (r), 149 (tl), 149 (br), 150, 151, 152, 153, 154, 155 (t), 155 (b), 156-7, 158-9, 160-1, 162, 163 (t), 163 (b), 164 (l), 165 (bl), 165 (tr), 168-9, 170-1, 172-3, 174 (tr), 174 (br), 175 (br), 175 (tr), 176 (br), 176 (tr), 177 (tl), 177 (br), 178 (t), 178 (b), 179 (tr), 179 (bl), 180, 181, 182, 183, 184-5, 186 (t), 186 (b), 187, 188, 188 (t), 192, 193, 194-5, 196, 197 (l), 197 (r), 198 (l), 198 (r), 199 (l), 199 (br), 200 (tl), 200 (br), 201 (tl), 201 (br), 202, 203 (l), 203 (tr), 204 (l), 204 (r), 205 (t), 205 (b), 206 (l), 206 (r), 207, 208 (l), 208 (r), 209 (t), 209 (b), 210, 211, 212, 213 (l), 213 (r), 214-5, 217(b), 217 (t), 222-3, 224, 226, 226 (t), 228 (l), 228, 229, 230 (t), 230 (b), 231 (t), 231, 232 (l), 232 (r), 233 (b), 233 (t), 234 (t), 235 (bl), 235 (r), 237 (b), 236, 237 (t), 238, 239 (t), 239 (b), 240-1, 242-3, 244-5, 246, 247 (t), 247 (b), 248, 249

Getty: 19, 30-1 (b), 49, 57 (t), 90 (r)

Mary Evans Picture Library: 11, 14 (l), 18, 20-1, 22-3, 24-5, 29, 31 (t), 36, 34-5, 46 (l), 64

Shutterstock: 48

Topham: 14-15, 22 (l), 26-7, 32-3, 34 (l), 37, 39, 58 (b), 59 (t), 82, 104 (bl), 107 (tl), 136 (tr), 216

Author Biography

Robert Jeffery is a writer and editor who lives in Surrey and supports AFC Wimbledon. His work has appeared in FourFourTwo, The Mail on Sunday, The Sunday Times, NME and When Saturday Comes, among others. He is the author of The Pictorial History of English Football (2001) and text editor of The Rough Guide To Cult Football (2003).

INDEX